# MANAGEMENT CASE STUDIES
## A STUDENT'S HANDBOOK

**Dr. Ramesh R Kulkarni, Dr. Shrinivas R Patil, Rajashekhar R Navalagi, Rangappa K Yaraddi**

INDIA • SINGAPORE • MALAYSIA

# Notion Press

Old No. 38, New No. 6
McNichols Road, Chetpet
Chennai - 600 031

First Published by Notion Press 2018
Copyright © Rangappa K Yaraddi 2018
All Rights Reserved.

ISBN 978-1-64324-309-2

Dedicated to
Teachers, Students and entire education fraternity.

# CONTENTS

## CASES ON FINANCIAL MANAGEMENT

## CASES ON HUMAN RESOURCE MANAGEMENT

# PREFACE

Teaching management is a challenge as compared to other disciplines of humanities and social sciences. Since management as a subject in classroom takes roots from various fields of study viz, mathematics, statistics, economics, psychology, communication, accountancy, commerce and various other related discipline. Along with conceptual knowledge, it is also required to teach the practical aspects of business to students, by giving latest and relevant illustrations from business and industry.

Therefore, teachers in management field uses variety of teaching methods like Power point presentations, Video lessons, Simulations, Projects, Management games, Field visits, Indoor and outdoor projects, Group discussions, Assignments and the most popularly case study methods. It is proved in many instances that, out of all the above methods of teaching, case study method is the most effective as it gives a textual picture of business situation or illustration as a standing example to teach various management concepts in class room with a very little expense and resources consumption.

Most popular business schools like IIMs, IBS, and Harvard Business School have been using case study method of teaching as a fundamental method in management education. Ravi Mathai the founder director of IIM in his book Brick by Brick mentions that, the teaching force of IIM was developed by training them on case study method of teaching by deputing them to Harvard. Even now, IIMs use case study as a fundamental method of teaching.

Case method is very effective and powerful teaching aid for teachers to develop real world professional skills of students. In a teacher and student-center teaching strategy, case study method can impart students with critical thinking, communication, and interpersonal skills. Learning management necessitates students work through complex, ambiguous, real world problems engages students with the course material, encouraging them to "see it from an action perspective, rather than analyze it from a distance" (Angelo & Boehrer). Case studies are, by their nature, multidisciplinary, and "allow the application of theoretical concepts…bridging the gap between theory and practice" (Davis & Wilcock).

Working on cases not only promotes students in their organizational skills but also in time management skills. Case method increases student proficiency with written and oral communication, as well as collaboration and team-work. "Case studies force students into real-life situations," training them in managerial skills such as "holding a meeting, negotiating a contract, giving a presentation, etc" (Daly, 2002).

Equally, teachers require good communication skills in using case study to teach in class. Teaching with case needs the teacher to be a moderator of the emerging ideas and thoughts. A basic frame work for case method is discussion on the concepts and contents of the case. He first needs to provoke students' thinking process on the direction of the case. Further brainstorm them to reveal the facts of the case and the concepts hidden in it. In turn, he has to instigate students' creativity, and conceptualizing skills out of a situation. Hence it needs a great deal of concentration by the teacher in the class room. Therefore an attempt is made in this text to propose a standard process of solving a case study from both the teacher and students point of view in the first chapter.

Another objective of this book is to facilitate teachers in picking up a right case for the class. Picking a right case is a challenge. A Good case study focuses on one issue or problem, and has a clear problem statement. Generally cases are narratives, situations, select data samplings, or statements that present unresolved or provocative issues, situations, or questions. The information included must be rich enough to make the situation credible, but not so complete as to close off discussion or exploration. Cases can be short for brief classroom discussions or long and elaborate for semester-long projects. Teacher shall choose a case that matches the course objectives, and which allows the students to apply what they learn in the course to the scenario. The most powerful and interesting cases are those that allow for several assessments of the same situation, leading to several equally plausible and compelling conclusions, each with different implications for action. Therefore authors have thought to provide a glossary of cases which can be picked to teach various aspects of management such as Finance, Marketing and HR. In the bargain 30 case studies have been developed keeping in mind to provide a quick pick of cases study for a management classes.

We hope this small effort of writing case studies to facilitate both teachers and students of management to teach and learn through case studies will be fruitful and widely used in future.

While writing this case study book, we have got tremendous help from industry, students and fellow colleagues. We are very much thankful to them towards their contribution in completing this book successfully. We thank all those, who have helped us directly and indirectly in writing this book.

– Dr. Ramesh R Kulkarni, Dr. Shrinivas R Patil,
Mr. Rajashekhar R Navalagi, Mr. Rangappa K Yaraddi

# GUIDELINES
# FOR SOLVING CASE STUDY

# GUIDELINES FOR SOLVING CASE STUDY

Every case is a story told with certain facts and figures of an organization either out of original published data facts or hypothetical presentation of a business situation. As such every case let has a general appearance and most of the times does not confine to a specific management concept. In general a case study can be viewed from more than one management perspective. In particular one case can be used to teach the multiple concepts in Marketing, and as well as supply chain management or strategic management in general. Rather it depends upon the teacher, as to how to use the case in teaching management concepts.

The art of solving the case depends upon the expertise of the teacher to explore the case and moreover depends upon his or her ability to articulate and relate the case to a particular management concept. Thus the key in solving a case study lies with the teacher himself. The best possible approach to adopt is to explore the students understanding on the case and further to relate his understandings from the case to the management concepts. This can be achieved by using probing technique to explore the ideas in the minds of the student by asking questions by brainstorming. The intelligence lies in proper sequencing of the questions probed. It should be more an interaction between the teacher and the students than solving the case in a mono delivery.

However for the benefit of the beginner teachers and students, a comprehensive case solving methodology has been discussed here below:

**How to solve the case study: (Step by step or procedural approach)**

This procedure has different logical steps. A different procedural step to find the best possible solution for the case is as follows.

1. **Read the case:** At the outset the students or teachers whoever solving the case must read the case carefully between the lines, until the story or gist of the case is understood. Twice or thrice reading is not bad as it is required to develop an understanding on the story, facts and events inside the case. While reading the case it is wise to underline the important lines showing facts and figures in the case with a pencil. So that, such an underlining provides a quick reference to the facts and figures covered in the case.

2. **Read the questions:** Once the case study is read, a quick look on the questions asked in the case may be read and understood as to what the case is all about and what concepts are expected to be

answered from the case. This enables the person to develop a grip on the concepts covered in the case and the story inside the case study.

3. **Identify the facts:** In this step identify the facts of the case and note down all the important facts from the given case let.

4. **Identification of the problem:** From the different facts noted, identify the problems/Issues associated with the case. In some cases multiple problems or issues may be there in a single case let.

5. **Define the boundaries:** In this step specify the limits under which case let has to be solved. Sometimes these limits will be given in the case let clearly else you need to assume the boundaries for the given case.

6. **Assumptions:** In some case lets you may notice the gaps in the data given. While noting the facts you have to fill such gaps by making assumptions. Assumptions made should be clearly stated along with the reasons.

7. **Develop the solutions for the case:** In this stage one should develop a solution, in this stage one should justify why this solution is best for the given case let and how it will be helpful for the given situation in the case let. It may be single solution or mixture of more than one solution. Listing of competencies of the best possible solution will be an added advantage.

8. **Managerial applications:** In this step one should explain clearly which managerial theories and concepts are applied to get the solution for the given case let?

9. **Conclusion:** In this step one can summaries the entire case let problems, action plan on optimal solution and implementation plane of the best solution optimally.

# MODEL CASE STUDY WITH SOLUTION

# ELECTRONICS RETAIL STORES

## RN Electronics Stores

RN Digital Retail Company has total 15 large format, and 5 small formats of electronics retail stores in Mumbai, Maharashtra, India. Company started first electronic retail store in the year 2013. Store-A was launched in the year 2015 in M-Mall and Store-B in the year 2016 in P-Mall. M-Mall & P-Mall have been positioned in two different strategic location of the city. Since the launch, both the stores have been struggling to meet the budgeted targets. Store-A measures 3000 sqft in size and has 30 employees including store manager, and department managers. Store-B measures 2800 sqft in size and has 25 employees including store manager, and department managers.

P & M Mall stores have mobiles and laptops as the assortments. Mobiles ranging from basic to high-end smart phones and laptops ranging from basic configuration to high-end gaming laptops are available in both the stores.

Mobile Assortments

    a.  Basic phones

    b.  Android Smartphones

    c.  Non Android phones

    d.  Mobile Accessories

Laptop Assortments

    a.  Basic usage

    b.  Business

    c.  High-end

    d.  Desktop

    e.  Computer Accessories

Both the stores A & B of RN Digital Retail Company have average 16% walk-ins of the mall.

Following tables show the store conversion from total walk-ins of the mall.

**Table No. 1:** M-Mall, RN Store Walk-In Report 2016 & 2017

| M-Mall – Store A | 2016 | | 2017 | |
|---|---|---|---|---|
| Month | Mall Walk-Ins | Store Walk-Ins | Mall Walk-Ins | Store Walk-Ins |
| July | 65,000 | 9,750 | 70,000 | 10,500 |
| August | 75,000 | 13,500 | 90,000 | 16,200 |
| Sept | 80,000 | 9,600 | 95,000 | 11,400 |
| October | 85,000 | 16,150 | 100,000 | 19,000 |
| November | 65,000 | 11,700 | 120,000 | 21,600 |
| December | 75,000 | 11,250 | 90,000 | 13,500 |

**Table No. 2:** P-Mall, RN Store Walk-In Report 2016 & 2017

| P-Mall – Store B | 2016 | | 2017 | |
|---|---|---|---|---|
| Month | Mall Walk-Ins | Store Walk-Ins | Mall Walk-Ins | Store Walk-Ins |
| July | 45,000 | 6,750 | 60,000 | 9,000 |
| August | 55,000 | 9,900 | 70,000 | 12,600 |
| Sept | 65,000 | 7,800 | 85,000 | 10,200 |
| October | 85,000 | 16,150 | 95,000 | 18,050 |
| November | 65,000 | 11,700 | 85,000 | 15,300 |
| December | 65,000 | 9,750 | 70,000 | 10,500 |

Electronic stores enjoy great sales during festivals and monsoon seasons hence; there were special offers and discounts for customers at RN Store of P-Mall. This activity helped store to increase the walk-ins.

M-Mall Store had ups and down in store profitability and P-Mall Store has consistently maintained positive store profitability, however has not achieved budgeted target. M-Mall store does an average of Rs. 1.18 crores sales on monthly basis, whereas P-Mall store does Rs. 1.30 crores average sales.

**Table No. 3:** Product-wise Sales from July to December 2017 of M-Mall RN Store

| M-Mall | Sales in lac (Rs) | | | | | |
|---|---|---|---|---|---|---|
| Products | Jul-17 | Aug-17 | Sep-17 | Oct-17 | Nov-17 | Dec-17 |
| Mobiles & Accessories | 31.09 | 37.82 | 39.63 | 43.59 | 41.61 | 37.65 |
| Laptop & Accessories | 83.41 | 121.06 | 67.68 | 74.45 | 71.07 | 64.30 |
| Grand Total | 114.50 | 158.87 | 107.31 | 118.04 | 112.68 | 101.95 |

**Table No. 4:** Product-wise Sales from July to December 2017 of P-Mall RN Store

| P-Mall | Sales in lac (Rs) | | | | | |
|---|---|---|---|---|---|---|
| Products | Jul-17 | Aug-17 | Sep-17 | Oct-17 | Nov-17 | Dec-17 |
| Mobiles & Accessories | 31.09 | 34.03 | 37.65 | 41.41 | 39.53 | 43.30 |
| Laptop & Accessories | 91.75 | 139.22 | 74.45 | 83.38 | 89.34 | 78.17 |
| Grand Total | 122.85 | 173.25 | 112.10 | 124.80 | 128.87 | 121.47 |

An experienced manager who recently quit managed P-Mall store. Hence it is now managed the department manager who has been with RN Digital Retail Company for more than 5 years. Since the store is located in Mall, there has been staff poaching from other company by offering better salary packages.

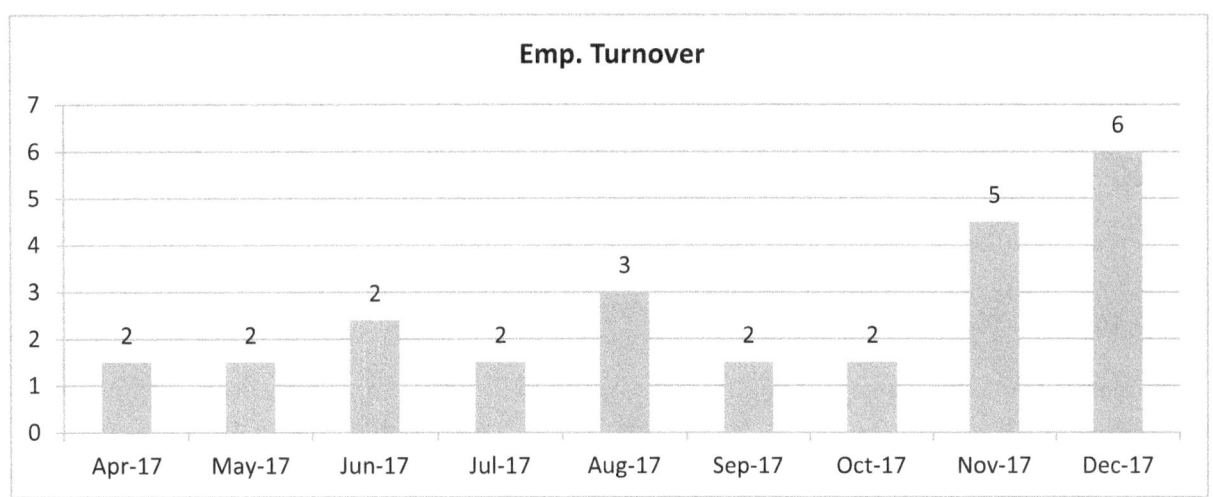

**Graph No. 1:** Employee Turnover of M-Mall RN Store, April to December 2017.

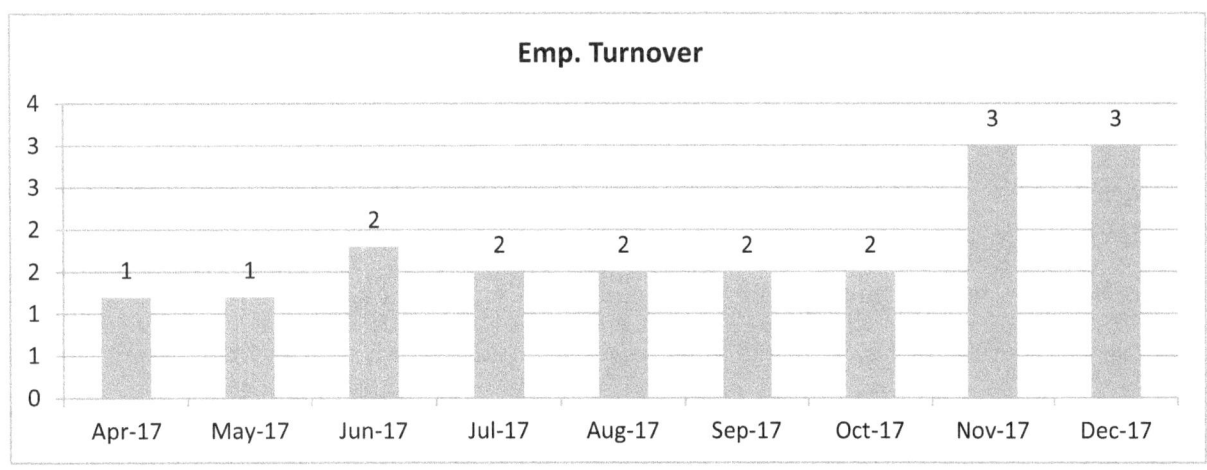

**Graph No. 2:** Employee Turnover of P-Mall RN Store, April to December 2017.

Considering the overall performance of both the stores, RN Digital Retail Company top management is fathoming about how to revive the performance of both the stores.

# SOLUTION TO THE CASE STUDY

Following steps help you to solve case study in a systematic approach.

## Step No-01 & 3: Read the Case and Identify the Facts

In this step identify the facts of the case and note down all the important facts from the given case let.

### Solution for Step No-01 & 3

1. Two electronics stores based at shopping malls launched in a time gap of one year.

2. Average sq.ft size of 2900.

3. Store walk-ins vs. Mall walk-ins stand at 16%.

4. Mobiles and laptops are the assortments of both the stores.

5. Different interventions to draw walk-ins by both the stores

6. Both the stores A & B of RN retail have average 16% walk-ins of the mall.

7. Special offers and discounts for customers at RN Store of P-Mall to generate sales.

8. M-Mall store does an average of Rs. 1.18 crores sales on monthly basis, whereas P-Mall store does Rs. 1.30 average sales.

9. There has been staff shuffling and 30% of the total store staffs are new.

10. Average employee turnover of 10% in Store A-M Mall, and 6% in Store B-P Mall.

## Step No-02 & 4: Read the Questions & Identification of the Problem

From the different facts noted, identify the problems/Issues associated with the case. In some cases multiple problems or issues may be there in a single case let.

## Solution for Step No-02 & 4

1. Poor walk-in conversion

2. Poor Sales

3. Employee turnover

# Step No-05: Define the Boundaries

In this step, specify the limits under which case let has to be solved. Sometimes these limits will be given in the case let clearly else, you need to assume the boundaries for the given case.

## Solution for Step No-05

The case is confined to Mumbai, Maharashtra, India with a scope of retail industry in the Mumbai city.

# Step No-06: Assumptions

In some case lets, you may notice the gaps in the data given. While noting the facts you have to fill such gaps by making assumptions. Assumptions made should be clearly stated along with the reasons.

## Solution for Step No-06

1. Employee conversion data is not provided in the case study, hence it is assumed, and those overall walk-ins into sales conversion are low across all employees.

2. Location of the stores in the shopping mall is not mentioned; hence, it is assumed that stores are not located in strategic place of the mall.

3. Employee turnover graphs do not specify role-wise attrition; hence it is assumed that a graph depicts attrition of frontline staffs.

4. A product mix sale is not provided hence it is assumed that P-Mall store has low sales contribution of high margin mobiles and laptops.

# Step No-07: Develop the Possible Solutions for the Case

In this stage, one should develop as much as solution one can give and each solution should give detail advantages and disadvantages.

**Solution 1:** "Relocation of stores within the Mall/Renegotiate Rental"

Both the stores have low walk-ins as compared to mall walk-ins. This indicates stores have low share of walk-ins, hence RN electronics to initiate talk with Mall management for either relocation of the store within the mall or renegotiate the rental.

i.  Advantages of solution no 1:

    a. **Relocation–**

        i.  This helps stores to move to a location where walk-ins can be increased.

        ii.  Increased walk-ins help store staffs for better conversion.

        iii.  Increase in conversion helps in increased Sales.

    b. **Renegotiate Rental –**

        i.  This helps stores to reduce rental cost.

        ii.  If walk-ins and Sales remain same, stores can make positive EBITDA.

ii.  Disadvantages of the solution 1:

    a.  Relocation of stores comes with huge expenditure of movement of fixtures, and stocks.

    b.  Increased marketing expenses post relocation, to create awareness.

    c.  No guarantee that new location helps in increase in walk-ins as expected.

**Solution 2:** "Marketing activities to increase walk-ins"

By RN Digital Retail Company–

RN Company has to launch marketing activities to draw attention of customers staying near the mall, so that walk-ins to the mall increase.

    a.  Glowing sign board at the entrance

    b.  Human banners

    c.  Paper insertion of Pamphlets

In Co-ordination with Mall–

List of activities include, DJ nights, Comedy shows, & Musical Nights by famous singers etc.

    i.  Advantages of solution no 2:

        a.  Increased awareness

        b.  Increased walk-ins

    ii.  Disadvantages of the solution 2:

        a.  Increased marketing expenses can have impact on store P&L.

**Solution 3:** "Walk-In Conversions"

Sales depend on how best front line staffs convert walk-ins into sales. Activities like Sales training and trackers help stores for increasing the walk-in conversions.

Training–

Each staff should undergo rigorous sales training wherein they should be trained to understand importance of customer.

Tracker–

A tracker should be placed in the stores so that each employee's performance is tracked basis total customers attended vs. converted.

   i. Advantages of solution no 3:

     a. Development of Customer Service Skills of staffs

     b. Improved quality Customer Service

     c. Increased Efficiency

     d. Through trackers, there will be increased accountability among staffs.

   ii. Disadvantages of the solution 3:

     a. Considering employee attrition, ensuring efficiency is difficult.

     b. Increase in cost of training because of attrition.

**Solution 4:** "Employee Turnover"

   a. Both the stores are not reaching the incentive slab, hence special slab for both stores to be set, so that employees can start earning incentive.

   b. Employee feedback mechanism to address their concerns

i. Advantages of solution no 4:

   a. Special incentive slab helps staffs to earn incentive, increased motivation, and morale.

   b. Re-configuration helps new hires to learn products and provide best customer service under the guidance of experience and expert staffs.

ii. Disadvantages of the solution 4:

   a. Non-performers might misuse the feedback mechanism.

   b. Demotivation for experienced & expert staffs if stores do not achieve target.

**Solution 5:** "Product Mix"

Following graphs depicts contribution of Mobiles & laptops to total sales.

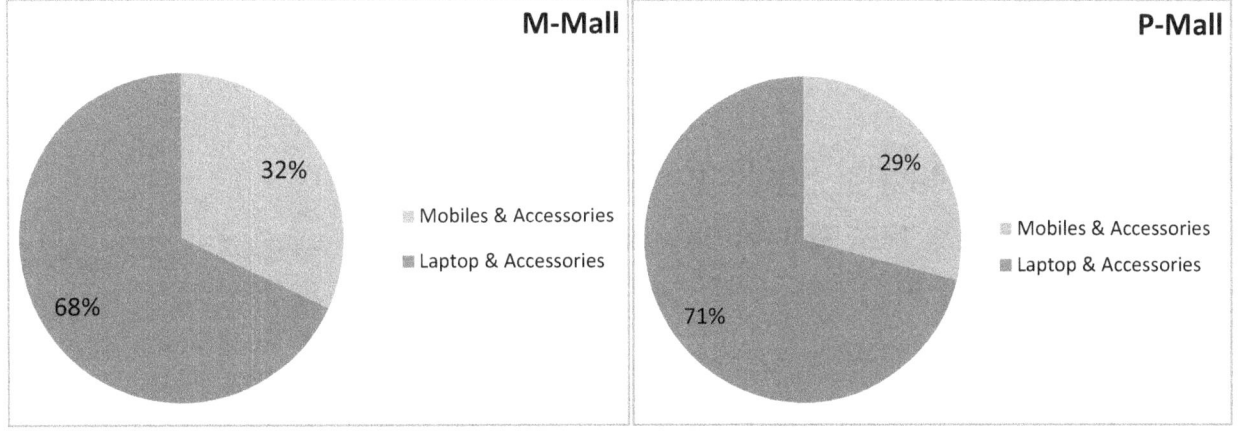

Mobiles of M-Mall store have more than P-Mall store, which is a good sign. Both stores to relook at product mix so that major focus should be on high margin products as well as high footfall generators. Like Android Smartphones in the price range of Rs. 8000 – Rs. 12000.

    i. Advantages of solution no 5:

        a. Increase in footfalls

        b. Increase in Sales

        c. Increase in Margin

        d. Positive impact on store P&L

    ii. Disadvantages of the solution 5:

        a. Decrease in store average bill value due to Mid-range priced mobiles

# Step No-07(A): Recommending the Best Possible Solutions

In this stage, one should justify why this solution is best for the given case let and how it will be helpful for the given situation in the case let. It may be single solution or mixture of more than one solution. Listing of competencies of the best possible solution will be an added advantage.

## Solution for Step No-07(A)

Suggested solutions are as follows –

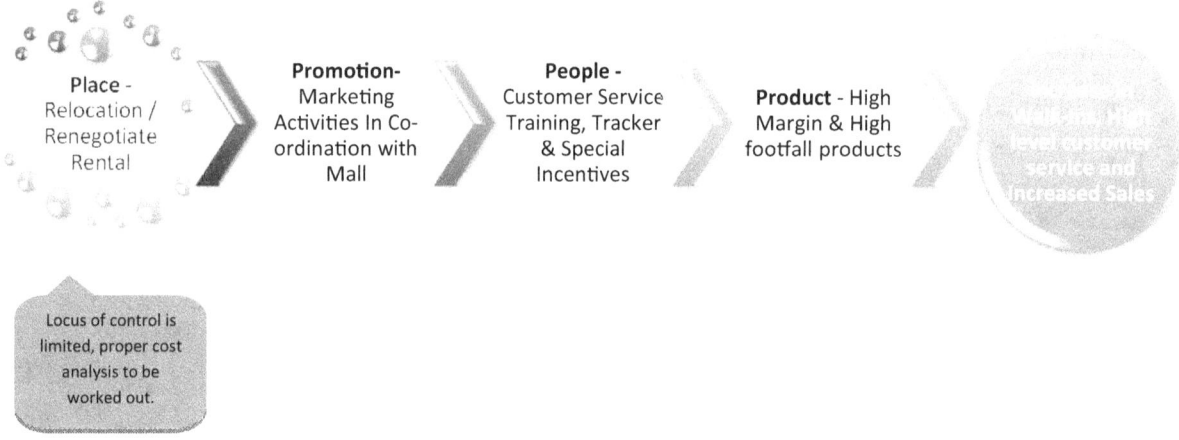

# Step No-08: Managerial Applications

In this step, one should explain clearly, which managerial theories and concepts are applied to get the solution for the given case let?

## Solution for Step No-08

4 P's of marketing has been used to the solution for the given case study.

# Step No-09: Conclusion

In this step, one can summaries the entire case let problems, action plan on optimal solution and implementation plan of the best solution optimally.

## Solution for Step No-09

Mall based stores of RN Digital Retail Company, Store A&B have been struggling with walk-ins and sales. Both stores have inadequate share of mall walk-ins. Low conversions and poor sales performance has led to low morale among employees. Hence it is recommended to relocate the store within the mall or Renegotiate Rental with mall management, Marketing Activities in Co-ordination with Mall like DJ nights, Comedy shows, & Musical Nights by famous singers etc.

Sales depend on how best front line staffs convert walk-ins into sales. Hence, activities like Sales training and trackers help stores for increasing the walk-in conversions. Both the stores are not reaching the incentive slab, hence special slab for both stores to be set, so that employees can start earning incentive. Relook at the product mix to increase footfalls, and margin.

# CASES ON GENERAL
# MANAGEMENT

# CELLPHONE & COMPUTER RETAIL STORES

## C&L – Company

C&L, Start-up Company has started its operation by venturing into retail stores with Mobile phones & Laptop exclusive stores. Management decided to open up 150 stores by 2014 all over India. Company appointed one of eminent person in the field of retail sector as its Chief Executive Officer (CEO). Immediately after assuming the office, CEO got into the action by recruiting Chief Operating Officer and other team to meet the objective set by the Board. Different departments were created to cater to different needs viz, Human Resource department to cater to people aspects, Business development to identify strategic locations, Marketing department to drive walk-ins and sales, Sales operations department to manage day to day store operations, standards and Sales, etc.

Business development team profile includes identifying store locations for the company. Company has tied up with top consultant to conduct catchment analysis. Business development team briefed consultant about the requirement of catchment. Catchment should be a strategic one, which has major business presence, type of households, ratio of rented vs. own houses, income level of the people staying, qualification and profession, type of business prevailing in the area, number of government offices, competition presence, business of existing outlets, etc is studied and arrived at potentiality of the location. Consultant conducted extensive catchment study and presented list of strategic locations.

Business Development team approached respective property owners to initiate the discussion to open up store. Business Development & Legal team verified all required legal documents and CEO, COO, and Business head visited each location to corroborate and certify locations to go ahead with signing an agreement with property owners.

By 2014, company opened 50 stores in Mumbai. Size of store ranges from 1000 to 2500 sq. ft. Employee strength varies from store to store basis size and locality of the store. A Store Manager, assisted by two supervisors and 5 to 8 front-end executives, manages each store. Assortment of store includes, mobile phones ranging from Basic to high-end, Laptops, and Accessories of Mobile and Laptops.

Company penetrated to growing markets like Ahmadabad, Baroda, Surat, Kolkata, Delhi, Bangalore, Hyderabad, Chennai, and Cochin by the end of 2014.

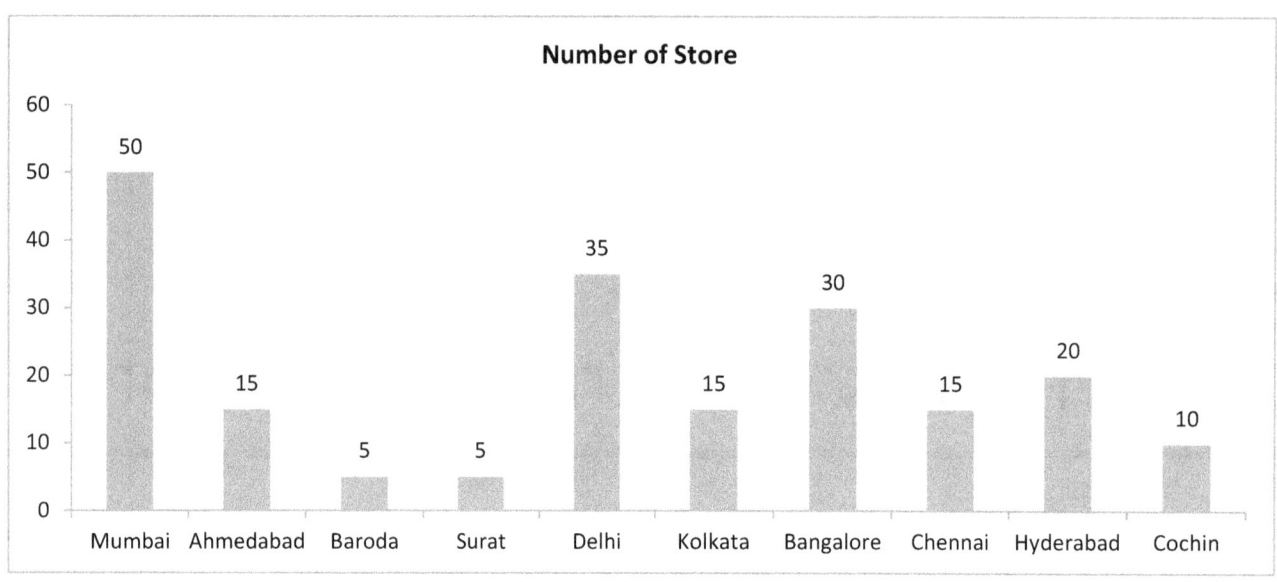

**Graph No. 1:** Number of Stores of C&L Company by 2014

Company over achieved the target of opening the stores. With growing number of stores, company management decided to add required employees at different levels. Following graphs show total customer support executives, supervisors, store managers deployed at each stores and number of Area managers managing the city.

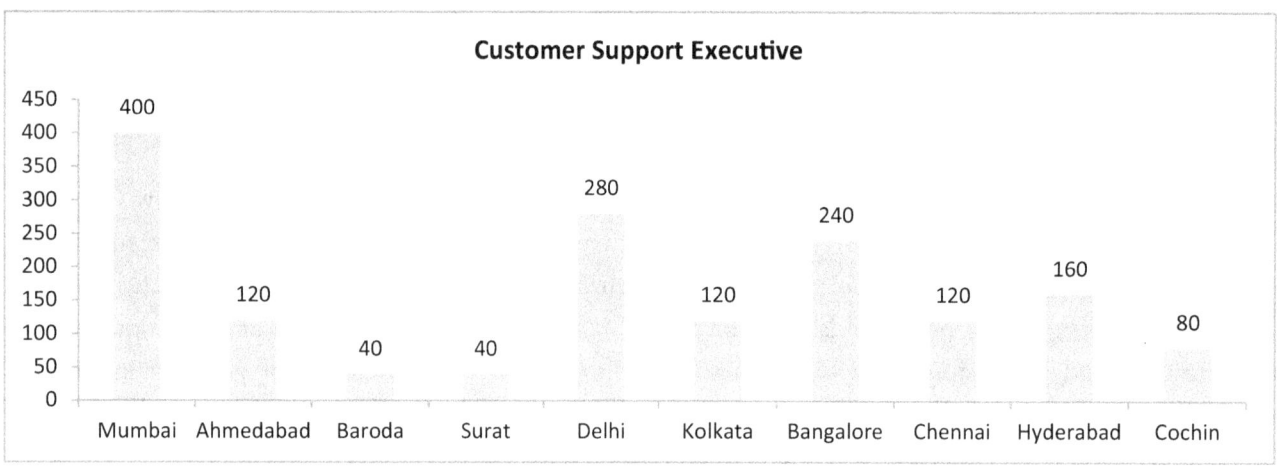

**Graph No. 2:** Number of Customer Support Executives city wise

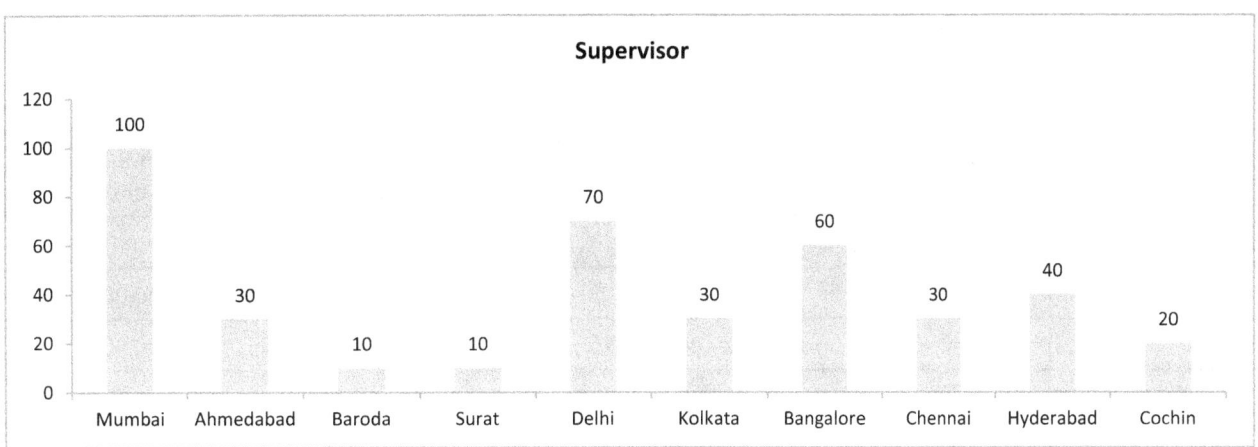

**Graph No. 3:** Number of Supervisors city wise

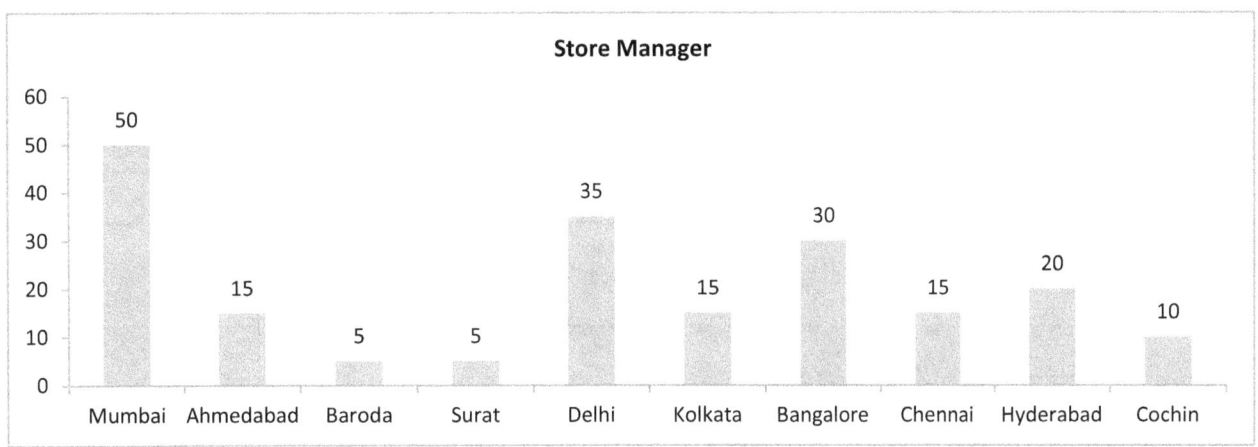

**Graph No. 4:** Number of Store Managers city wise

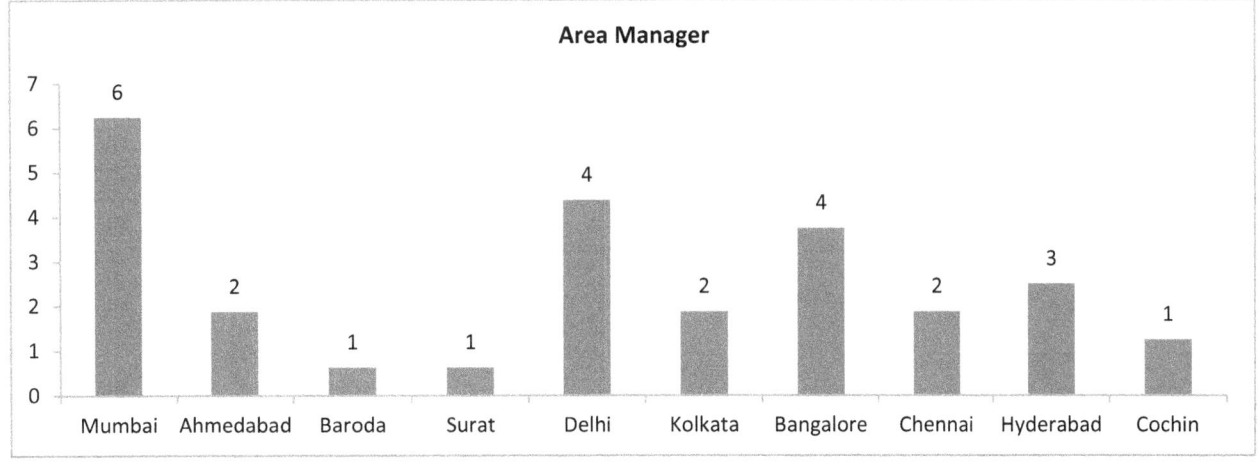

**Graph No. 5:** Number of Area Manager City wise

Average employee cost to the overall sales is at 5.5% for 2015, and 2016. Company is known for its employee oriented policy, and work environment.

**Table No. 1:** Average CSE & Supervisors Compensation per month

| City | Customer Support Executives | | Supervisors | |
|------|-----------------------------|---|-------------|---|
| | No. of Employees | Total Compensation per month | No. of Employees | Total Compensation per month |
| Mumbai | 400 | 3,200,000.00 | 100 | 1,200,000.00 |
| Ahmedabad | 120 | 720,000.00 | 30 | 300,000.00 |
| Baroda | 40 | 240,000.00 | 10 | 100,000.00 |
| Surat | 40 | 240,000.00 | 10 | 100,000.00 |
| Delhi | 280 | 2,240,000.00 | 70 | 840,000.00 |
| Kolkata | 120 | 720,000.00 | 30 | 240,000.00 |
| Bangalore | 240 | 1,680,000.00 | 60 | 720,000.00 |
| Chennai | 120 | 840,000.00 | 30 | 300,000.00 |
| Hyderabad | 160 | 1,120,000.00 | 40 | 480,000.00 |
| Cochin | 80 | 480,000.00 | 20 | 160,000.00 |
| **Total** | **1600** | **11,480,000.00** | **400** | **4,440,000.00** |

**Table No. 2:** Average Store Manager & Area Manager Compensation per month

| City | Store Manager | | Area Manager | |
|------|---------------|---|--------------|---|
| | No. of Employees | Total Compensation per month | No. of Employees | Total Compensation per month |
| Mumbai | 50 | 750,000.00 | 6 | 593,750.00 |
| Ahmedabad | 15 | 180,000.00 | 2 | 103,125.00 |
| Baroda | 5 | 60,000.00 | 1 | 28,125.00 |
| Surat | 5 | 60,000.00 | 1 | 28,125.00 |
| Delhi | 35 | 525,000.00 | 4 | 393,750.00 |
| Kolkata | 15 | 180,000.00 | 2 | 103,125.00 |
| Bangalore | 30 | 420,000.00 | 4 | 281,250.00 |
| Chennai | 15 | 210,000.00 | 2 | 121,875.00 |
| Hyderabad | 20 | 280,000.00 | 3 | 150,000.00 |
| Cochin | 10 | 140,000.00 | 1 | 62,500.00 |
| **Total** | **200** | **2,805,000.00** | **25** | **1,865,625.00** |

To manage day-to-day operations of stores, company has flat organisation structure in place. Along with Sales team, other functional team like HR, Marketing, Finance to ensure adherence to process, standards at each store and achieve sales target set by the company.

**Table No. 3:** City wise Number of Regional employees

| Roles/City | Mumbai | Ahmadabad, Surat & Baroda | Delhi | Kolkata | Bangalore | Chennai | Hyderabad | Cochin |
|---|---|---|---|---|---|---|---|---|
| Regional Marketing Manager | 1 | 1 | 1 | 1 | 1 | 1 | 1 | 1 |
| Marketing Executives | 5 | 4 | 4 | 2 | 3 | 2 | 2 | 1 |
| Regional Human Resource Manager | 1 | 1 | 1 | 1 | 1 | 1 | 1 | 1 |
| HR Executives | 5 | 4 | 4 | 2 | 3 | 2 | 2 | 1 |
| Regional Administration Manager | 1 | 1 | 1 | 1 | 1 | 1 | 1 | 1 |
| Regional Finance Manager | 1 | 1 | 1 | 1 | 1 | 1 | 1 | 1 |
| Finance Executives | 5 | 4 | 4 | 2 | 3 | 2 | 2 | 1 |
| IT Executives | 2 | 3 | 2 | 1 | 2 | 1 | 1 | 1 |

Following is the corporate team based at Delhi.

**Table No. 4:** Number of Corporate office employees

| Roles/City | Corporate Office |
|---|---|
| Head of Marketing | 1 |
| Head of Sales | 1 |
| Head of Buying | 1 |
| Head of HR | 1 |
| Head of Finance | 1 |
| Head of IT | 1 |
| Buying Team | 50 |
| Marketing Team | 20 |
| Finance Team | 30 |
| Human Resource Team | 15 |
| IT Team | 15 |

Presence of both national & local players created huge competition. Increased competition gave rise to increased real estate cost, marketing expenses and employee cost. Rental cost stands at 6% of the overall sales for the company with average Rs. 142 per sq.ft.

In recent report published by C&L Management, following is the Sales and Store EBITDA from 2014 to 2017.

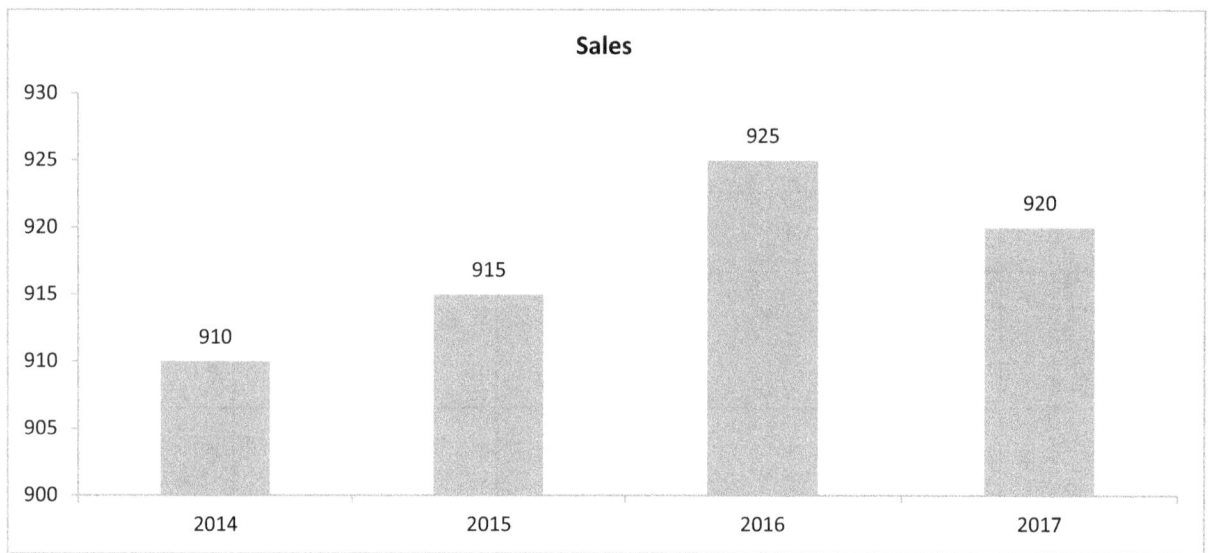

**Graph No. 6:** C&L Sales from 2014 to 2017

**Graph No. 7:** C&L Store EBITDA from 2014 to 2017

Report of C&L management highlighted that, the area where company can leverage upon are margin, and space on hire. Considering overall performance, C&L company board has decided to take corrective measures before it is too late. Board has suggested, Chief Executive Officer (CEO) and Chief People Officer (CPO) to reduce rental and lay off employees. Board is of the view that these are only two areas to correct and revive the company performance. CEO and CPO are worried about impact of layoff on employees and company brand image.

# A CASE ON PRINCIPAL OF MANAGEMENT

The president of TSH Infrastructure ltd sat at his chair, after working hours of the office. A thought was going on in his mind about Alex who is a purchase manager and his ability to work with Vishal, the marketing and sales manager of TSH Infrastructure ltd.

When a purchase department was established in September 2015; Vishal and other department heads agreed with the need of purchase department which will centralize the functions with a specialist in-charge. Vishal was of the view that inflow of materials in to the firm was important enough to take any new assignments professionally. Purchase department began operating, it is been precisely the marketing and sales manager who have had a issue with the new purchase manager in regard to the way the purchase department is carrying out its functions. The purchase department has developed a formal set of procedure that has resulted a time commitment of all departments including marketing and sales department. Further Vishal is specially irritated by the fact that his need for particular specification is constantly being questioned by the purchase department. This has hurt the ego of Vishal. Because he assumes that purchase manager job is to fulfill the needs of other departments not to question them.

Vishal has expressed a strong opinion in front of President many times that, 'the purchasing function is an integral part of marketing function' their fore need to be managed jointly. Alex has worked in the purchase department of the firm previously which was considerably bigger then TSH Infrastructure ltd. He was interviewed by all the top managers including Vishal before being hired. But it was President who negotiated the offer of job details. Vishal believes that Alex is somehow subordinate to him.

| Half yearly results in brief of TSH Infrastructure ltd | | | | | (Rscrore) |
|---|---|---|---|---|---|
| | Sep' 16 | Mar' 16 | Sep' 15 | Sep' 14 | Sep' 13 |
| Raw material | 115.29 | 141.53 | 166.06 | 303.79 | 223.49 |
| Other income | 6.23 | 9.67 | 8.95 | 8.14 | 3 |
| Employee expenses | 11.54 | 13.91 | 14.14 | 13.7 | 12.85 |
| Other expenses | 13.15 | 19.83 | 21.98 | 29.32 | 22.34 |
| Depreciation | 1.21 | 1.4 | 1.64 | 1.8 | 1.54 |

The different departments have complained about the details that purchase department requires on their requisition. But Alex has a documented proof that materials are now being purchased much more economically than before. Alex sees Vishal has no particular relationship between his responsibilities for efficient procurement; Vishal's job is to market the firm's products.

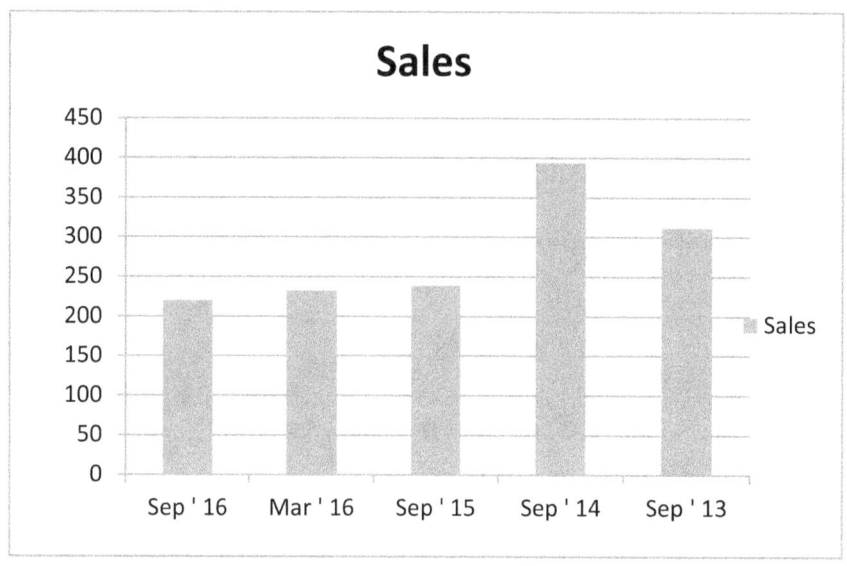

The President is very disturbed with the continuing conflict among two managers and much of his time is been taken up for this issue. The time has come to take some positive decision to sort out the conflict.

## Discussions

1. How do you evaluate Vishal's position as marketing and sales head?

2. Do you think that this conflict has association with factors of formal organization?

3. If you are the president of TMC Infrastructure ltd what will you do now.

# GRAPEVINE COMMUNICATION

A company called Umiyaji Corporation is making huge profit every year. The main reason for growth of the company at fast pace is because of its two employees Mr. Ramesh and Mr. Sam. Mr. Ramesh and Mr. Sam are both the project managers of the company. Both are equally capable, hardworking, and result oriented. They both have common nature i.e. meeting the deadline at any cost. They have good relation with the management of the company, employees and with everyone. The position in the company or the salary doesn't matter to them. But Mr. Ramesh is from a rich family and his father is a minister in the ruling party. The company has decided to promote one of them to the post of Vice president of the company. The management of the company called both of them and spoke about the promotion, both said that it doesn't matter whom the company promotes as meeting the deadline of the task is important for them.

As the news of promotion spread, rumors also started, a rumor was spread that Mr. Ramesh's father is pressurizing for his promotion and Mr. Sam is threatening to quit if he is not promoted. It was the hot matter of discussion for the employees. This news spread even to management. Due to this rumor Mr. Sam was distracted from his work. To add to it management took a decision to promote Mr. Ramesh in its annual function. Then the rumor became very dominant. Mr. Sam also couldn't work well as the employees were not responding as earlier. Six months later Mr. Sam resigned for his post and joined the new construction company as project manager in Jan 2016. The company profit started declining. The financial details of the company is shown in the below table.

| Quarterly results in brief of Umiyaji Corporation | | | | | (Rscrore) |
|---|---|---|---|---|---|
| | **Mar'15** | **Jun' 15** | **Sep' 15** | **Dec' 15** | **Mar' 16** |
| Sales | 195.56 | 248.39 | 284.08 | 272.54 | 174.62 |
| Operating profit | 57.05 | 35.69 | 66.95 | 69.85 | 18.96 |
| Interest | 35.38 | 28.46 | 18 | 48.91 | 41.4 |
| Gross profit | 27.11 | 18.46 | 71.15 | 20.39 | -7.91 |
| EPS (Rs) | 7.96 | 2.67 | 17.09 | 4.01 | -6.34 |

## Discussions

1. Analyze the problem. How would you tackle the problem if you are the HR manager of the company.

2. What steps you suggest to regain the profit status of Umiyaji Corporation.

# REDUCTION OF WORK FORCE

Mr. Akhil is a senior HR Manager Production division of reputed MNC based in Noida. Akhil was been in the company since its inception. Last month Akhil was part of the executive board meeting in which overall cost reduction was an issue for the company. One option that was explored was to significantly reduce human capital cost. Akhil was very much aware it is important to balance business considerations with employees who may lose their job after many years loyal to the company.

Table shows a brief Quarterly results between March 2014–2015

| Quarterly results in Brief | | | | | (Rscrore) |
|---|---|---|---|---|---|
| | Mar' 14 | Jun' 14 | 14-Sep | Dec' 14 | Mar' 15 |
| Other income | 5.44 | 11.24 | 23.2 | -0.55 | 14.54 |
| Raw material | 113.19 | 184.81 | 169.43 | 172.93 | 120.25 |
| Employee expenses | 13.9 | 14.86 | 25.53 | 19.49 | 19.95 |
| Other expenses | 9.44 | 11.03 | 22.47 | 10.27 | 14.46 |
| Depreciation | 8.81 | 9.26 | 5.31 | 11.84 | 12.32 |
| Taxation | -1.96 | 2.41 | 22.35 | -2.39 | -4.09 |
| Net profit/loss | 20.25 | 6.79 | 43.49 | 10.21 | -16.14 |
| Extra ordinary item | - | - | - | -0.72 | - |
| Equity capital | 25.45 | 25.45 | 25.45 | 25.45 | 25.45 |

At the same time Akhil is concerned about performance of the employees, ethical issues and long term success of the organization. He knows that road ahead will be rough in which he has to walk. It is his responsibility as well to ensure the organization moves in the right direction with care in order to maintain profitability.

While the production sector is the growing market, the company did not shift to appropriate production practice and was unable to adopt new technology. Company has lost revenue and market share from last two quarters due to competition, inappropriate product focus and misaligned sales force incentives. Sales in the market are down by 32%. Disappointing second quarter results had forced the management to conduct a executive board meeting to discuss the current status and future strategy. To regain market share management believes that proper production practice and adoption of suitable technology are the key areas of concern. This could include a shift in human capital expertise. Management is appropriately nervous that to regain company market position in a reasonable time frame.

The graph shows sales of the company in the period of 2014–2015 FY.

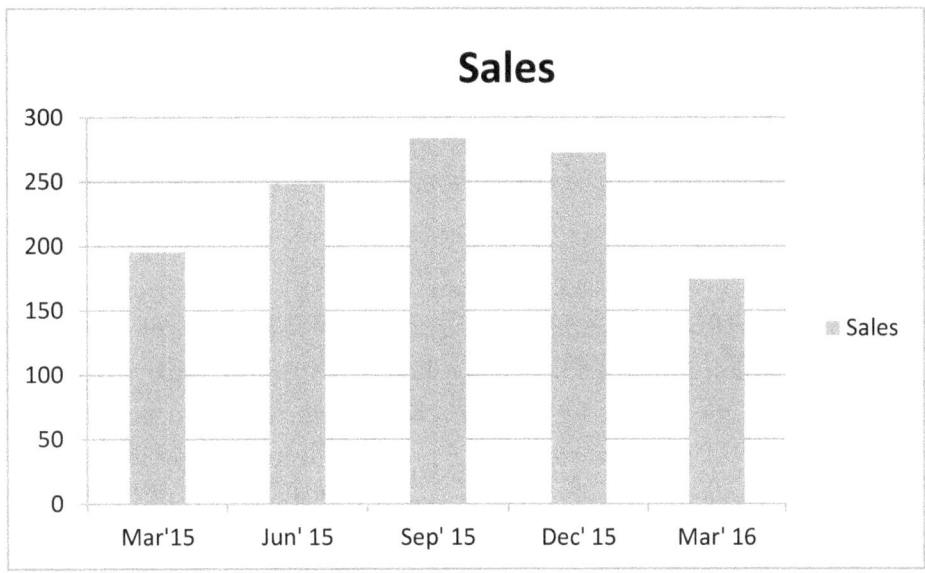

The executive's team has determined that the production unit should reduce human capital cost by 15%. This cost was determined by calculating annual salary of the employees and other cost such as training, employees benefits etc. Akhil encourage the team to consider the number of different options. He believes that offering of early retirement packages is one of the best ways to reduce the cost and still produce favorable outcome for employees. Generally this packages offer the attractive package for employees to encourage them to leave the organization. In addition company would pay 100% health care benefits for 10 years.

In short term this may be an expensive approach. Mean while company may lose many of its senior employees and the organization knowledge they posses.

## Discussions

1. What would you recommend as a best reduction strategy?

2. If you are the employee of the organization would you accept the early retirement package of the company? Justify.

3. Discuss the Akhil's stand on the situation.

# MANUFACTURING MONOPOLY

Bharat steel ltd is a Chennai based steel manufacturing company. It has enjoyed market preference for its products due to less competition in the field. Usually there will be more orders than what the company could produce. But the situation changed quickly because of entry of two new competitors with the foreign collaboration in the field. The company faced problems in marketing its steel products with the usual profit margin. Some of the dealers who are associated with Bharat steels ltd prefer other company products as profit margin is higher.

Sensing the likely problem the Managing Director appointed Mr. Sumankumar as a General Manager to direct the operations of the production division. After taking a charge as General Manager Mr. Sumankumar got the briefing from all the departments. He asked all the heads to list out major problems and issues of their department.

Marketing department head indicated that in order to achieve higher sales, he need more sales force, and generous budget for teams which could be sent to customer place to win the business. Further there should be more profit margin to dealers as they can promote company products. The production head complained about old technology and equipments are used in manufacturing due to which cost of production was high. Competitors have better technology and equipments due to foreign collaborations. This made their products superior than Bharat Steel ltd. The head of purchase department complained about delayed payments to vendors due to which he could not supply the raw materials required on time for steel production.

| Annual results in brief (Bharat steel ltd) | | | | | (Rscrore) |
|---|---|---|---|---|---|
| | Mar' 17 | Mar' 16 | Mar' 15 | Mar' 14 | Mar' 13 |
| Sales | 1,509.66 | 1,661.28 | 1,756.59 | 1,585.42 | 1,569.31 |
| Raw material | 900.05 | 878.34 | 1,003.47 | 907.48 | 943.86 |
| Research and development expenses | - | - | - | - | - |
| Employee expenses | 100.26 | 98.26 | 82.06 | 75.06 | 75.86 |
| Other expenses | 400.52 | 481.85 | 479.95 | 433.9 | 414.3 |
| Operating profit | 100.41 | 191.65 | 169.28 | 147.01 | 118.46 |

At this moment Mr. Sumankumar has to take some positive action to bring back the original profit margin and sales, without any major capital outlay.

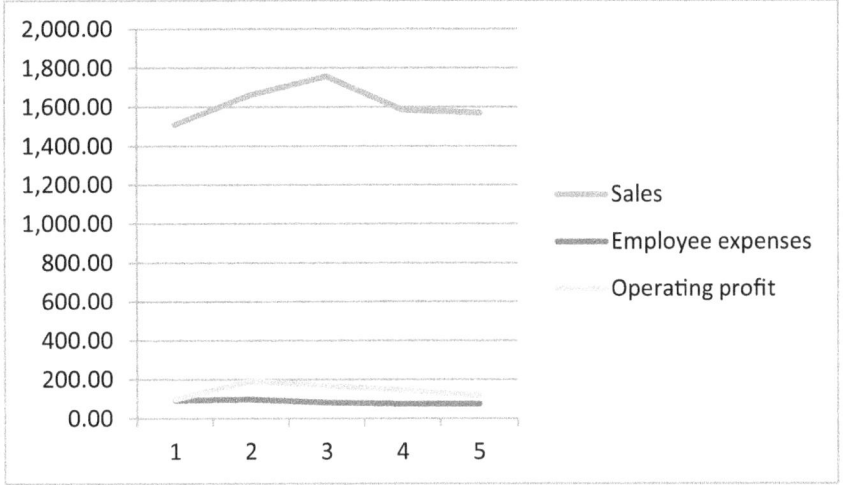

## Questions

1. Suggest the steps to overcome the problems in this case.

2. Discuss the nature of the problems in the case.

3. If you are The General Manager of the company, how will you handle the case?

# INVESTMENT IN NEW TECHNOLOGY FOR RETENTION OF CUSTOMER

Loyal Retail Mart is in to FMCG sector with 20 crore investment and has a presence in 25 cities of south India. The distribution network consists of authorized branches, franchises, and re-sellers. The company has a centralized database management system to maintain better customer relationship practices.

With a competition growing day by day, it is the experience of the customer with company's product and services, which matters the most and determines the company's profit margin and future. Those days are gone where one looks constantly for new potential customer ignoring the existing ones. It is very essential for the companies to keep the existing customers satisfied and continuously engaged. By serving to their satisfaction will generate more business through them and through their referrals.

The Loyal Retail Mart has hired a private research firm to conduct a market research about the different aspects of customer retention. Based on the market research they were able to get the below facts about Loyal Retail Mart. That highlights the importance of customer retention. The management of Loyal Retail Mart wants to make investment in e-CRM, as a strategy towards better customer retention. The financial details of Loyal Retail Mart are shown in the following tables.

| Annual results in brief of Loyal Retail Mart | | | | (Rscrore) |
|---|---|---|---|---|
| | Mar' 16 | Mar' 15 | Mar' 14 | Mar' 13 |
| Sales | 11.34 | 3.45 | 5.13 | 5.02 |
| Operating profit | 0.38 | -0.19 | 0.25 | 0.25 |
| Interest | 0.02 | 0.01 | 0.08 | 0.36 |
| Gross profit | 0.45 | -0.2 | 0.17 | -0.1 |

| Liquidity ratios | | | | |
|---|---|---|---|---|
| | Mar' 16 | Mar' 15 | Mar' 14 | Mar' 13 |
| Current ratio | 6.18 | 5.01 | 2.17 | 2.36 |
| Current ratio (inc. st loans) | 6.18 | 4.9 | 2.17 | 2.36 |

| Liquidity ratios | | | | |
|---|---|---|---|---|
| | Mar' 16 | Mar' 15 | Mar' 14 | Mar' 13 |
| Quick ratio | 4.53 | 2.96 | 1.16 | 1.25 |
| Inventory turnover ratio | 7.94 | 3.01 | 2.28 | 1.95 |

**Market research Statistics and facts:**

i. Price is not the main reason for customer attrition. It is actually due to the overall poor quality of customer services and grievance handling.

ii. A customer is more likely to defect to competitor, if the problem is services related rather than price or product related.

iii. The statistics shows non-satisfied customer will tell between 10–15 people about their experience.

iv. Satisfied customer whose issues are addressed within the time frame will tell to approximately 5 people, about their experience.

v. It costs 30%–50% more to acquire a new customer than retain the existing customer.

vi. The chance of selling to existing customer is 75%–85%. The chance of selling to potential customer is about 30%–50%.

vii. Satisfied customer will visit the store 40% more likely than others.

Following table gives a brief data of customer walk-ins in to Loyal Retail Mart (all 25 outlets) in Tire-I and Tire-2 cities put together for the year of 2015 and 2016.

**Table:** Walk-In Report for Loyal Retail Mart for the year 2015 & 2016 (Tire I and Tire II cities) all 25 stores put together

| Month | 2015 | | 2016 | |
|---|---|---|---|---|
| | Tire I cities | Tire II cities | Tire I cities | Tire II cities |
| July | 9500 | 6705 | 15020 | 8500 |
| August | 10500 | 9090 | 16330 | 11450 |
| Sept | 21000 | 7080 | 22010 | 10040 |
| October | 10800 | 16015 | 18010 | 16500 |
| November | 11300 | 11070 | 19500 | 15530 |
| December | 9900 | 9705 | 18030 | 13700 |

# Discussions

1. Based on the financial status of the company, will you suggest the company for the investment in new technologies?

2. How Loyal Retail Mart can understands the needs and expectations of customers by implementing e-CRM.

3. How e-CRM will help to build the better distribution network for Loyal Retail Mart with its franchise stores and resellers.

# CASES ON MARKETING MANAGEMENT

# ELECTRONICS RETAIL STORES

## RN Electronics Stores

RN Digital Retail Company has total 15 large formats, and 5 small formats of electronic retail stores in Bangalore. Company started first electronic retail store in the year 2013. Store-A was launched in the year 2015 in one of the strategic location of the city, MG Road. Store measures 6500 sqft in size and has 30 employees including store manager, and department managers.

Store is in the location, which is strategically located and it can draw a very good crowd on a daily basis. The Catchment area has income group ranging from Middle to High Income and with both individual houses and premium apartments. The luxury/premium apartments in the area are with more than 500 flats. Senior Executives, Professionals working in MNCs and businesspersons own majority of these flats. Around 50% of the houses of the area are on rented. Rental ranges from Rs. 15000 to Rs. 1 lakh. In addition, the area has the presence of two major shopping malls.

The stretch where the store is located has the presence of all branded stores from Apparel to Foot ware to Jewellary to Electronics to Restaurants. Two shopping malls of the area are the 'shopertainment' for customers because they offer mix of all types of products & services through major branded outlets and including multi-screen movie theatres and food under single roof. This makes them a week-end destinations for people of the area. The average space cost per sq.ft in the stretch ranges from Rs. 10,000 to Rs. 12,000 for residential and Rs. 125 – Rs. 150 per sq.ft rental for commercial buildings.

Following is the walk-in report published by RN Digital Electronics stores for 2014–15.

**Table No. 1:** Total Walk-Ins of the area & store walk-ins for 2014–15

| Month | 2014 | | 2015 | |
|---|---|---|---|---|
| | Total Walk-ins of the Catchment | Store Walk-Ins | Total Walk-ins of the Catchment | Store Walk-Ins |
| Apr | 123,750 | 18,563 | 165,000 | 24,750 |
| May | 148,750 | 26,775 | 175,000 | 31,500 |
| Jun | 153,000 | 18,360 | 170,000 | 20,400 |

*Contd.*

| Month | 2014 | | 2015 | |
|---|---|---|---|---|
| | Total Walk-ins of the Catchment | Store Walk-Ins | Total Walk-ins of the Catchment | Store Walk-Ins |
| Jul | 122,500 | 23,275 | 175,000 | 33,250 |
| Aug | 148,000 | 26,640 | 185,000 | 33,300 |
| Sep | 202,500 | 50,625 | 225,000 | 56,250 |
| Oct | 220,500 | 66,150 | 245,000 | 73,500 |
| Nov | 199,750 | 35,955 | 235,000 | 42,300 |
| Dec | 140,000 | 26,600 | 200,000 | 38,000 |

In 2014, Store had average of 1084 walk-ins on daily basis. In 2015, average walk-ins per day have increased by 21%.

There are 10 competitor stores in the radius of 5 km of the RN Digital store. 2–3 stores have national presence, whereas remaining stores are local players. Product assortment of all electronics including RN Digital store includes, LED TVs, Home theatres, Refrigerators, Washing Machines, Air Conditioners, Laptops, Smartphones, DSLR cameras, Microwave Ovens, Food Processors, Other Small appliances, and Accessories of major electronics products.

There is a stiff competition from two national players, like Digital Electronics Store & Electronics Destiny stores, which are located in the same area. With the same size and same assortment, the Digital store does more than the RN Digital store. Digital Electronics Store draws more walk-ins than the RN Digital store. In addition, RN Digital store faces competition from other local players located nearby malls. (Refer Table No-2: Competition Sales & Graph No-1: Market Share of the catchment).

**Table No. 2:** Competition Sales – 2015

| Month | Sales in Values (Cr) | | | | | |
|---|---|---|---|---|---|---|
| | RN | Digital Electronics Store | Electronics Destiny | Electronics Store | Home Store | Others |
| Apr-15 | 0.80 | 1.50 | 1.00 | 0.70 | 0.50 | 0.80 |
| May-15 | 0.85 | 1.75 | 0.75 | 0.70 | 0.45 | 0.65 |
| Jun-15 | 0.75 | 1.00 | 0.60 | 0.55 | 0.40 | 0.55 |
| Jul-15 | 0.80 | 1.50 | 0.65 | 0.55 | 0.47 | 0.50 |
| Aug-15 | 1.80 | 2.00 | 1.50 | 1.35 | 0.85 | 0.95 |
| Sep-15 | 2.00 | 2.10 | 1.75 | 1.55 | 1.30 | 1.45 |
| Oct-15 | 2.00 | 2.50 | 1.85 | 1.65 | 1.25 | 1.35 |
| Nov-15 | 1.90 | 2.30 | 1.65 | 1.45 | 1.25 | 1.35 |
| Dec-15 | 1.70 | 2.00 | 1.55 | 1.35 | 1.00 | 1.00 |

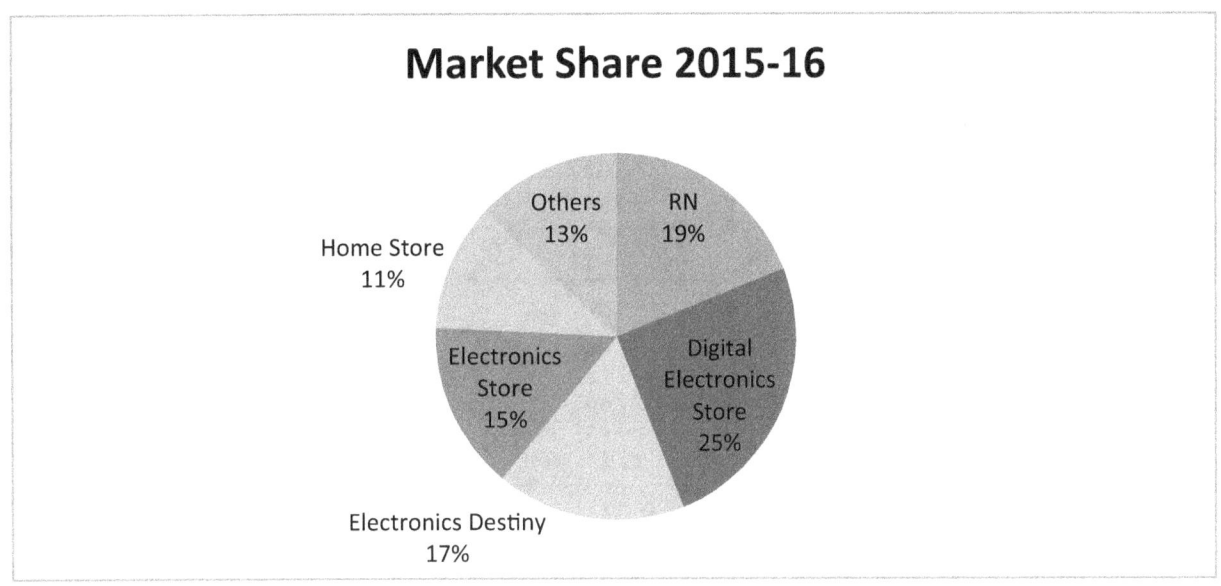

**Graph No. 1:** Market Share of the catchment 2015–16

Due to heavy competition in the catchment, sales staffs of RN Digital stores have been finding it difficult to convert walk-ins into sales.

Reasons quoted by sales staffs for low conversion are –

a. Customers take complete demonstration of the product because all major models of the brands are on display in RN Digital store.

b. At the time of closing the deal, they reject quoting as high price.

c. Demands for huge discount, which RN Digital company discourage.

d. Customer demands for offers or freebies.

e. Gold coin/Car as bumper prize by local players

f. Full-page paper Ads by Digital Electronics Store, Electronics Destiny & Other local players.

Electronic stores enjoy great amount of sales during festivals and monsoon seasons; hence, retailers offer special prices and discounts for customers. Beginning of August 2016, one of major online players came out with offers and huge discounts on electronics products as part of 'Festival Offers.' Offers were to the tune of up to 50% off on selling price of the product. There were exclusive products like Smartphones & Laptops available with huge price difference from the products available in the physical stores. The success of these offers boosted the morale of e-retailers and gave a big disappointment to sales of physical stores.

On October 2016, e-retailers launched massive offers for the customers on electronics products as part of the Diwali festival. Offers on selected electronic products were up to 90%. This has transformed the way customer shop electronic products. Eye catching offers lured customer attention towards online shopping. People found it more convenient to shop because they can see the product online, order it, and get it delivered at doorstep avoiding the trouble of moving from shop to shop in search of products. All this had major hit on Sales & Profit of Physical stores.

**Table No. 3:** Competition Sales – 2016

| Month | Sales in Values (Cr) | | | | | |
|---|---|---|---|---|---|---|
| | RN | Digital Electronics Store | Electronics Destiny | Electronics Store | Home Store | Others |
| Apr-16 | 0.68 | 1.28 | 0.85 | 0.60 | 0.43 | 0.68 |
| May-16 | 0.72 | 1.49 | 0.64 | 0.60 | 0.38 | 0.55 |
| Jun-16 | 0.64 | 0.85 | 0.51 | 0.47 | 0.34 | 0.47 |
| Jul-16 | 0.68 | 1.28 | 0.55 | 0.47 | 0.40 | 0.43 |
| Aug-16 | 1.53 | 1.70 | 1.28 | 1.15 | 0.72 | 0.81 |
| Sep-16 | 1.70 | 1.79 | 1.49 | 1.32 | 1.11 | 1.23 |
| Oct-16 | 1.70 | 2.13 | 1.57 | 1.40 | 1.06 | 1.15 |
| Nov-16 | 1.62 | 1.96 | 1.40 | 1.23 | 1.06 | 1.15 |
| Dec-16 | 1.45 | 1.70 | 1.32 | 1.15 | 0.85 | 0.85 |

The impact of e-retailers festive offers has on the sales mix of the RN Digital stores.

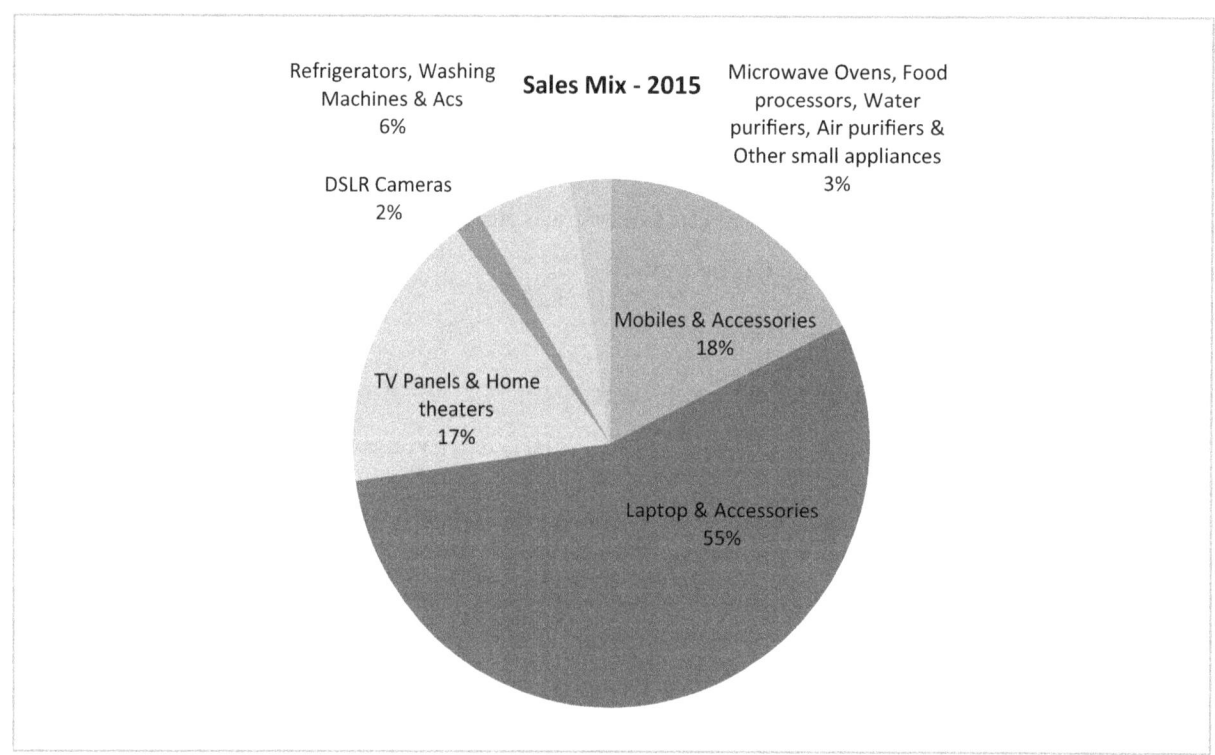

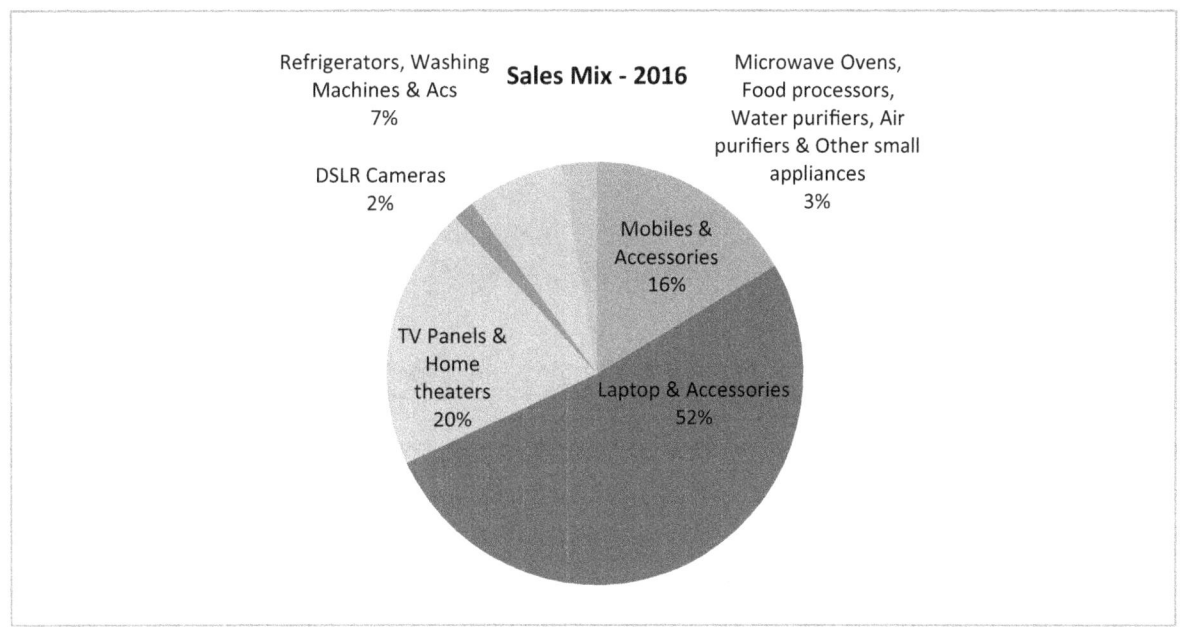

**Graph No. 2:** Sales Mix of RN Digital Store for October 2015 & 2016.

Sales staffs of RN Digital store at MG Road had tough time to convince customers on objections by the customers regarding prices offered by e-retailers, hence lost many potential customers. Exclusive smartphones & laptops by e-retailers and competitive prices for other mobile phones & laptops had major impact on these two products.

Changing customer expectations, increasing competition among physical stores, & e-retailers, increasing employee compensations, increasing rentals and decreased margins have impact on overall performance of physical stores. Considering all these factors and performance of the RN Digital store at MG Road, Top Management of the company has to relook at the strategies to survive to meet customer expectations, compete with other physical stores & e-retailers, and make margin to take company to profitability.

# INDIAN RURAL MARKET

Rural India is gaining importance. The fast moving consumer goods (FMCG) sector in rural and semi urban India is estimated to cross US $100 billion by 2025. The rural fast moving consumer goods market is expanding at a compound annual growth rate (CAGR) of 17.41 percent of US $100 billion during 2009–25. In terms of revenue 40% of the fast moving consumer goods market accounts from rural India.

India consists of about 650000 villages. These villages consist of about 850 million consumers making up for about 70 percent of the population and contributing around 50 percent of the Gross Domestic Product (GDP). India's per capita GDP in rural area has grown at a compound annual growth rate (CAGR) of 6.2 percent since 2000. The fast moving consumer goods (FMCG) sector in rural and semi urban India is expected to cross US $20 billion by 2018.

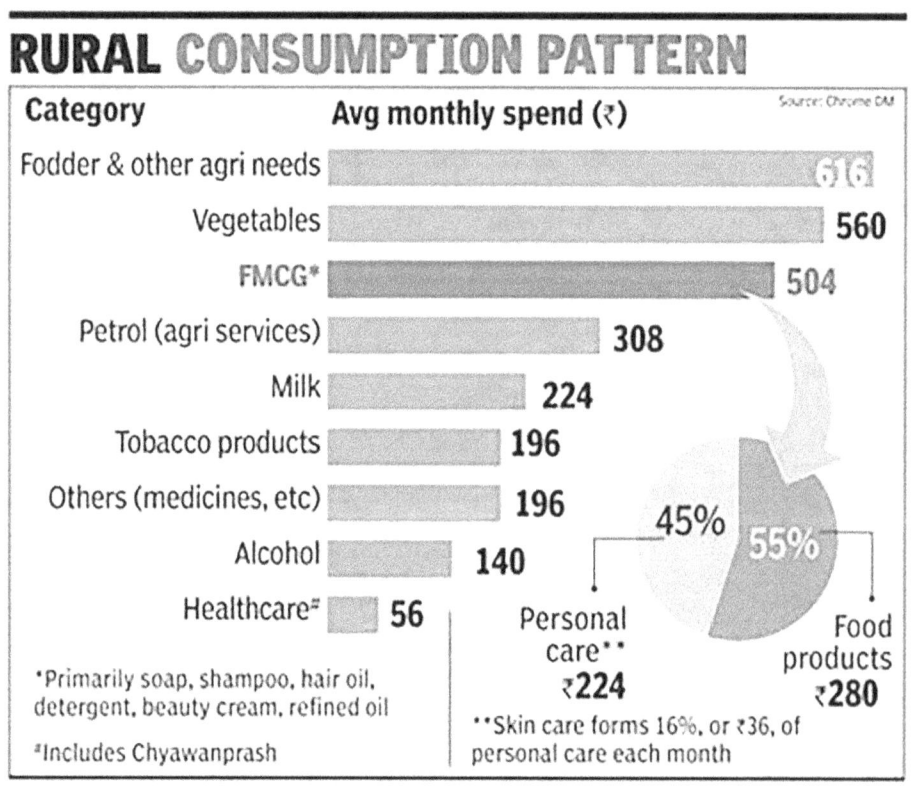

The above figure shows rural consumption pattern per month in 2016 in Indian rupees (source: Times of India)

The buying behavior and consumption pattern in rural market are gradually changing. More likely it resembles the consumption pattern of urban areas. These days' consumers from rural regions are also opting for online purchases. Over a period of time rural region consumption may go digitally.

As per the private research firm the internet users in India will cross 513.71 million by 2022. Fallowing statistics provides information on the number of internet users in India from 2015 to 2022 by a private research firm.

| Internet users in India from 2015 to 2022 by a private research firm. (Millions.) | | | | | | | |
|---|---|---|---|---|---|---|---|
| 2015 | 2016 | 2017 | 2018* | 2019* | 2020* | 2021* | 2022* |
| 259.86 | 295.30 | 332.7 | 371.09 | 410.6 | 449.88 | 483.56 | 513.71 |

"*" Indicates the projected numbers in millions.

Some consumer companies have their one-third customer from rural India. Rural regions are now witnessing increasing penetration of computer and smart phone with well covered basic telecommunication services. The internet has become cost effective. Private companies looking to overcome geographic barriers and broaden its area have additional advantages in rural region. Rural India provides large and attractive investment opportunities for private and foreign FMCG companies.

Below graph shows a Rural FMCG market trends in US $billions (Source: AC Nielsen, Dabur Reports)

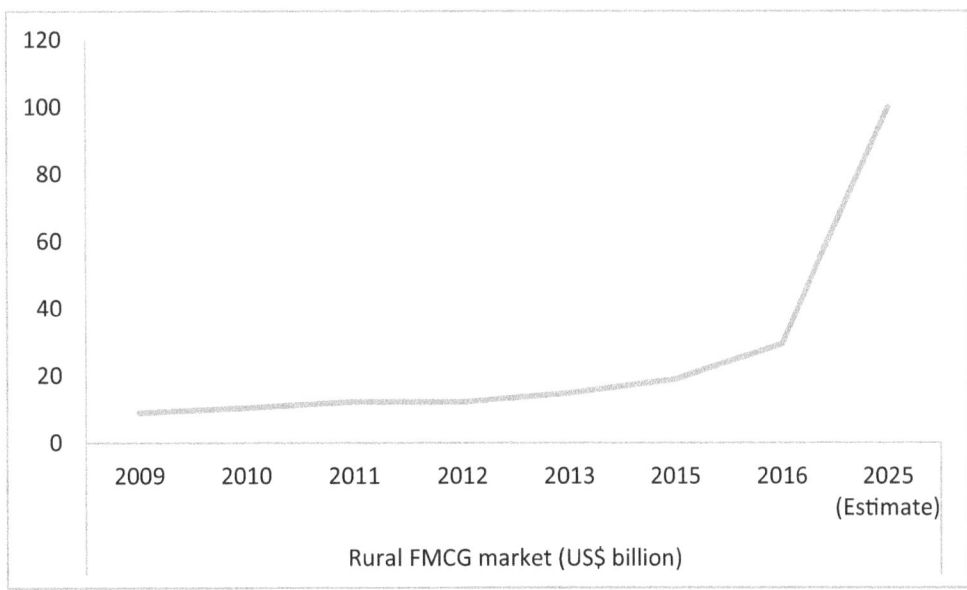

## Discussions on Case

1. How would you evaluate the rural FMCG market as an opportunity for E-Commerce companies in India?

2. Do you think an investment in rural market is viable in current scenario? Discuss in detail.

# RN SUPERMARKET

## RN Supermarket

RN Food Retail Company has total 100 supermarkets across India. In 2010, company expanded its operations to Bangalore, burgeoning market.

In 2011, company launched a new store in Mahatma Nagar. This area is a hub of recreational and commercial activity. It is the area with swanky shopping malls, shopping outlets of great brands and luxury apartments. The Catchment area has income group ranging from Middle to High Income and with both individual houses and premium apartments. The luxury/premium apartments in the area are with more than 1000 flats. Senior Executives, Professionals working in MNCs and businesspersons own majority of these flats. The area houses politicians and business tycoons.

There is a major competitor store in the radius of 2 km of the RN Supermarket. Area has ranges from high end branded outlets to small time kirana stores. There is a stiff competition from national player, like C1 Supermarket. With the same size and same assortment, the C1 supermarket does more than the RN Supermarket. C1 draws more walk-ins than the RN Supermarket. In addition, RN Supermarket faces competition from other local players located nearby the store. (Refer Table No-2: Sales & Graph No-1: Market Share of the catchment).

**Table No. 1:** Sales – 2011 and 2012

| Month | Sales in Values (lakhs) – 2011 | | | | | |
| | RN | C1 | C2 | C3 | C4 | C5 |
|---|---|---|---|---|---|---|
| Apr-11 | 0.50 | 0.60 | 0.40 | 0.38 | 0.33 | 0.35 |
| May-11 | 0.35 | 0.42 | 0.28 | 0.26 | 0.23 | 0.25 |
| Jun-11 | 0.30 | 0.36 | 0.24 | 0.23 | 0.20 | 0.21 |
| Jul-11 | 0.32 | 0.38 | 0.26 | 0.24 | 0.21 | 0.22 |
| Aug-11 | 0.40 | 0.48 | 0.32 | 0.30 | 0.26 | 0.28 |
| Sep-11 | 0.45 | 0.54 | 0.36 | 0.34 | 0.29 | 0.32 |

| | Sales in Values (lakhs) – 2011 | | | | | |
|--------|------|------|------|------|------|------|
| Month | RN | C1 | C2 | C3 | C4 | C5 |
| Oct-11 | 0.55 | 0.66 | 0.44 | 0.41 | 0.36 | 0.39 |
| Nov-11 | 0.45 | 0.54 | 0.36 | 0.34 | 0.29 | 0.32 |
| Dec-11 | 0.40 | 0.48 | 0.32 | 0.30 | 0.26 | 0.28 |
| | **3.72** | **4.46** | **2.98** | **2.79** | **2.42** | **2.60** |

| | Sales in Values (lakhs) – 2012 | | | | | |
|--------|------|------|------|------|------|------|
| Month | RN | C1 | C2 | C3 | C4 | C5 |
| Apr-11 | 0.53 | 0.63 | 0.50 | 0.45 | 0.39 | 0.42 |
| May-11 | 0.37 | 0.44 | 0.35 | 0.31 | 0.28 | 0.29 |
| Jun-11 | 0.32 | 0.38 | 0.30 | 0.27 | 0.24 | 0.25 |
| Jul-11 | 0.34 | 0.40 | 0.32 | 0.29 | 0.25 | 0.27 |
| Aug-11 | 0.42 | 0.50 | 0.40 | 0.36 | 0.32 | 0.34 |
| Sep-11 | 0.47 | 0.57 | 0.45 | 0.40 | 0.35 | 0.38 |
| Oct-11 | 0.58 | 0.69 | 0.55 | 0.49 | 0.43 | 0.46 |
| Nov-11 | 0.47 | 0.57 | 0.45 | 0.40 | 0.35 | 0.38 |
| Dec-11 | 0.42 | 0.50 | 0.40 | 0.36 | 0.32 | 0.34 |
| | **3.91** | **4.69** | **3.71** | **3.32** | **2.93** | **3.12** |

| | Sales in Values (lakhs) – 2013 | | | | | |
|--------|------|------|------|------|------|------|
| Month | RN | C1 | C2 | C3 | C4 | C5 |
| Apr-11 | 0.51 | 0.69 | 0.55 | 0.49 | 0.43 | 0.46 |
| May-11 | 0.33 | 0.49 | 0.38 | 0.34 | 0.30 | 0.32 |
| Jun-11 | 0.27 | 0.42 | 0.33 | 0.29 | 0.26 | 0.28 |
| Jul-11 | 0.27 | 0.44 | 0.35 | 0.31 | 0.28 | 0.30 |
| Aug-11 | 0.38 | 0.55 | 0.44 | 0.39 | 0.35 | 0.37 |
| Sep-11 | 0.45 | 0.62 | 0.49 | 0.44 | 0.39 | 0.42 |
| Oct-11 | 0.55 | 0.76 | 0.60 | 0.54 | 0.48 | 0.51 |
| Nov-11 | 0.38 | 0.62 | 0.49 | 0.44 | 0.39 | 0.42 |
| Dec-11 | 0.29 | 0.55 | 0.44 | 0.39 | 0.35 | 0.37 |
| | **3.41** | **5.16** | **4.08** | **3.65** | **3.22** | **3.44** |

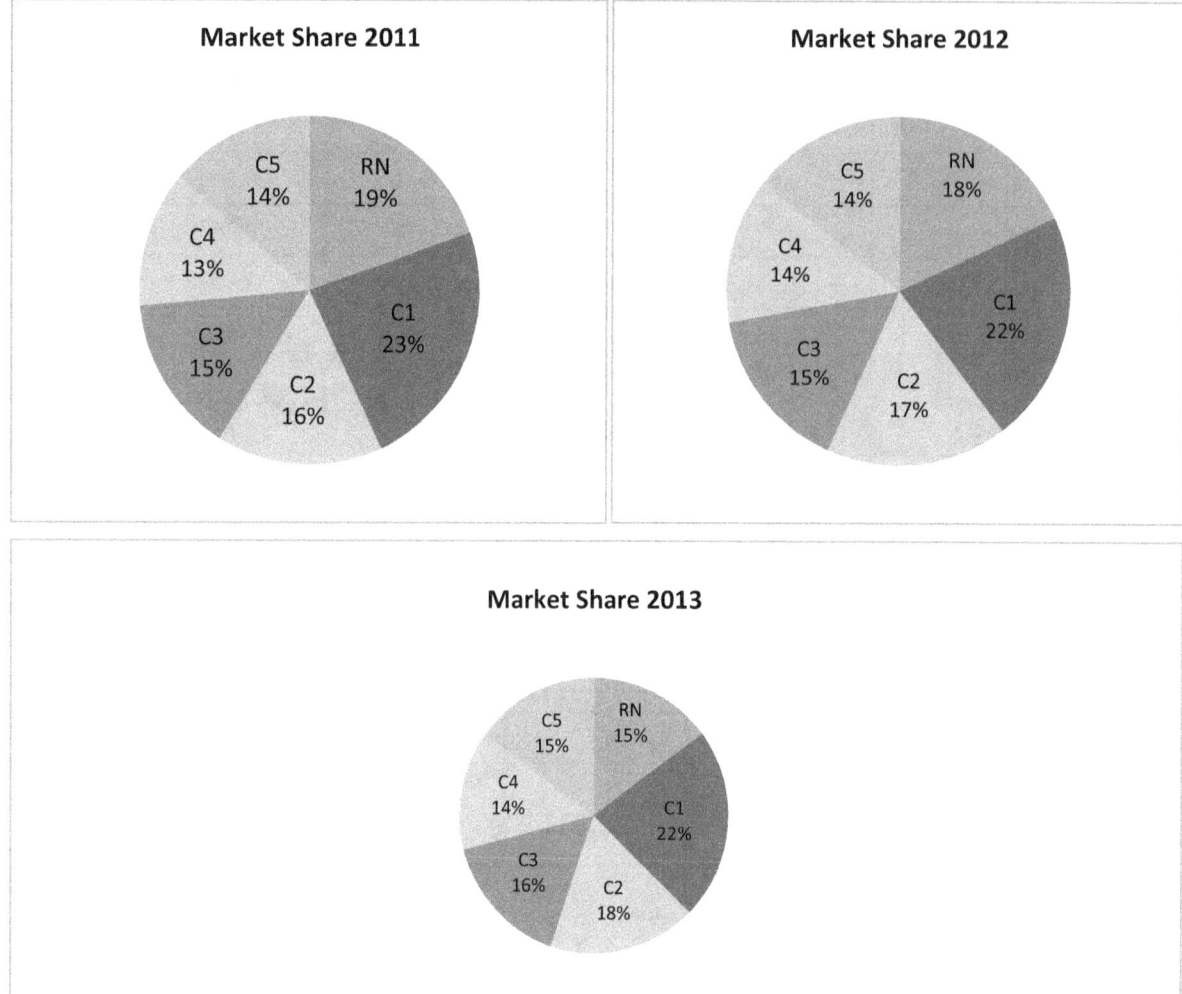

**Graph No. 1, 2 & 3:** Market Share of the catchment 2011, 2012 and 2013

Overall market has witnessed huge growth in sales because of growing households in the area and area is becoming a major shopping destination for customers. Both national & local players have shown good growth in sales for 2012. Seeing the potential of the catchment, many other retail outlets have been mushrooming with specialized in products viz, exclusive Fruits & Vegetable stores, Grocery stores, etc.

Store measures 2000 sq.ft in size and has following assortment–

a. Fruits & Vegetables

b. Staples

c. Home Needs

d. Food & Beverages

e. Home care

f. Personal care

A Store Manager heads RN Supermarket, 2 supervisors and 15 customer service staffs support him. Store Manager comes with 10 years of experience in food & grocery industry. He is with RN Food Retail Company for 5 years. He has replaced a Store Manager, who worked from the launch of store to until May 2012. There have been many changes in supervisors. Since the launch, there has been huge attrition in Supervisors & Customer Service Staffs' (Refer Graph No.4 – Employee Turnover 2012 and 2013)

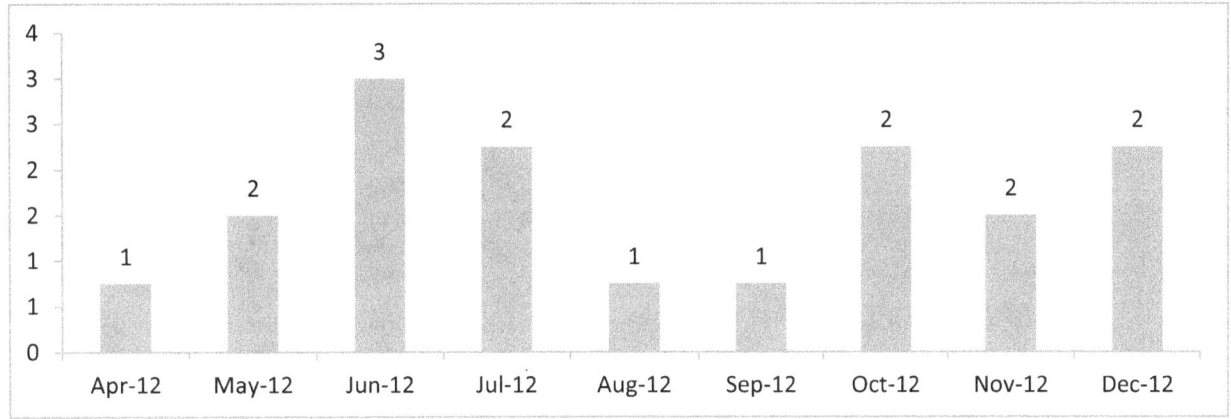

**Graph No. 4:** Employee Turnover 2012

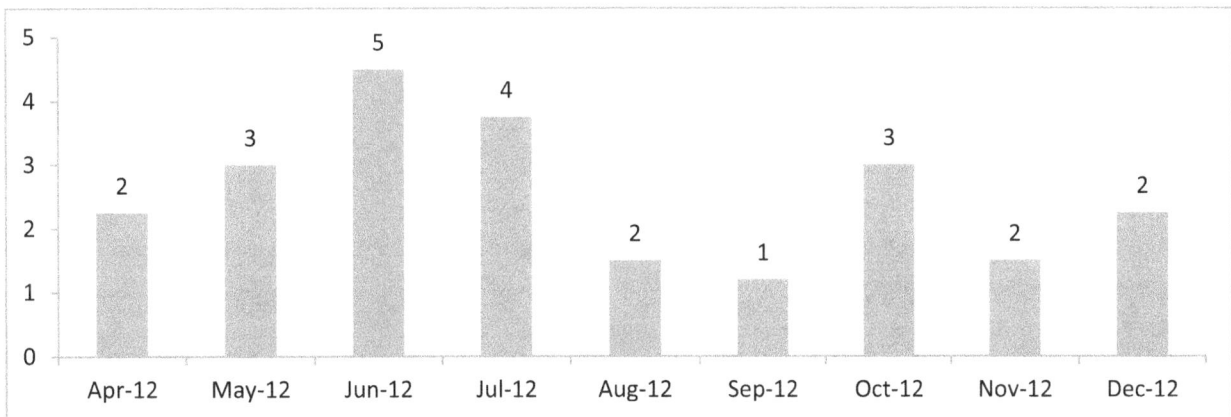

**Graph No. 5:** Employee Turnover 2013

Supervisors of the store who worked so far have been in the retail industry for last 5 years, with graduation as the qualification. Customer service staff comes with 1 or 2 years of with or without retail experience and with SSLC/Matriculation as the qualification. Store Manager & Supervisor of the supermarket gets salary package based on his/her experience. RN Food Retail Company pays Rs. 15000 to Rs. 20000 per month for Store Manager, Rs. 8000 to Rs. 12000 for Supervisors, Rs. 5000 to Rs. 6000 for Customer Service Staffs. With every year appraisal system in place, average hike per employee is at 7% to 10% except Customer Service Staffs. However, there is huge salary disparity among retail outlets in the area.

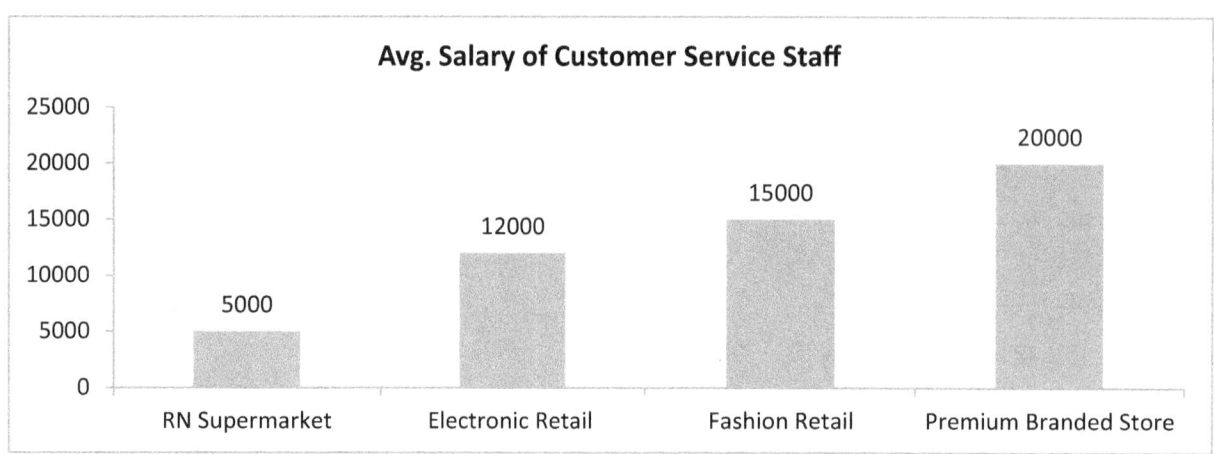

**Graph No. 6:** Average salary of Customer Service staff (Author own compilation)

City is growing with swanky shopping malls, customer lifestyle is changing and the catchment is growing with many branded outlets, however RN Supermarket is witnessing huge competition, decrease in sales and bulging employee turnover.

# DILEMMA AT AIBS LOGISTICS

## Introduction

Logistics is viewed as the foundation of the economy as it guarantees productive and practical stream of merchandise and other business segments rely upon it. Logistics industry in India is developing quickly. It is the interaction of framework, innovation and new sorts of specialist organizations, which characterizes whether the logistics business will have the capacity to enable its clients to decrease their expenses and give powerful administrations. In spite of feeble reaction, the logistics business keeps on seeing development attributable to the advance in retail, online business and assembling parts. As per the private research firms, the Global Logistics part was relied upon to grow 10 to 15% in 2013–14. Logistics industry is relied upon to reach over $2 billion by 2019. Ascent of online business logistics and expanded household utilization will make ready for the business to become advance in future. With the guarantee of unfaltering development and change, the administration situated logistics industry is prepared to extend past the skylines in the last 50% of this decade.

## Recent Scenario

The current Indian logistics area contains inbound and outbound fragments of the assembling and administrations supply chains. Recently, the logistics foundation has picked up the truly necessary lift from business houses and in addition strategy creators. Dealing with the foundation to adequately rival different enterprises has not been given its due accentuation. Deficient logistics framework can make bottlenecks in the development of an economy. The logistics administration regimen has the capacity to beat the detriments while giving bleeding edge intensity over the long haul. There exist a few difficulties and open doors for the part in the Indian economy.

## Difficulties Faced By the Recent Logistic Industry in India

The greatest test looked by the business today is poor coordination of transport systems, data innovation and stockroom and appropriation offices. Directions existing at various levels are forced by national, provincial and nearby specialists. Be that as it may, the controls contrast from city to city, blocking the production of national systems. Prepared labor is basic for the outsider logistics area and the assembling and retailing segments. It is missing at the IT, driving and stockroom and additionally at the higher vital level. The part is in a muddled state in India. The general view of logistics being a labor driven industry and absence of sufficient preparing organizations have made emergency of gifted administration and customer benefit faculty. Poor offices and administration are explanations for large amounts of misfortune, harm of stock, predominantly in the perishable segment. The issue emerges predominantly as a result of the nonappearance of expert hardware, as legitimate coolers. Absence of value preparing is another reason. In spite of the fact that professionals and academicians are gradually getting to be plainly mindful of the significance of logistics and inventory network, in any case, the field is as yet not sufficiently investigated the extent that examination is concerned. It is basic to organize innovative work with the goal that the shortcomings in the business can be dealt with and moved forward.

## About AIBS Logistics

AIBS Logistics is one of the leading logistics company with a net worth of 280 Cr. it provides all kind of logistics services across India with a total capacity of 400 vehicles. The vehicle range is from small capacity (1 ton) to large capacity (20 tons) are available with AIBS Logistics. AIBS logistics also has a facility to repair/modify the break down vehicles at its workshop. The workshop has rest room, claim petroleum bunk designated by Indian Oil Corporation, emanating treatment plant with limit of 1,75,000 liters, and rain water gathering plant. The complex has a vehicle benefit complex. Each truck in the fleet goes through this ace service facility in any event once at regular intervals.

AIBS Logistics has extended its activities into messenger administrations and express freight. AIBS Logistics handles more than 600 MT of bundles each day signifying 316,000 MT of payload for every year. With the biggest system in India, the AIBS Logistics distributes traverses 18 states in India and is bolstered by around 832 branches, 36 center points cum transport yards and around 2600 clients. With its own trans-shipment yard beginning activity at Delhi sooner rather than later, it is extending its administrations to cover area in other North Indian states.

AIBS logistics has started its tour operation division last year (2016) with 150 buses, in which 51 Volvo buses including a mix of 9400XL and 9400PX multi axle bus models on more than 100 routes across major tourist destinations. The operation is supported by a network of over 56 branches and more than 600 booking agents across country. The following table gives a brief description of the tour operation division of AIBS Logistics.

| 1 | Depots/administrative offices | 26 |
|---|---|---|
| 2 | Divisions | 3 |
| 4 | Vehicles | 150 |
| 5 | Schedules | 104 |
| 6 | Effective Kms per day | 39060kms |
| 7 | Average traffic revenue per day | Rs. 1623000. |
| 8 | Average passengers travelled per day | 3766 |
| 9 | Staff | 314 |

In recent days AIBS logistics management has noticed that at least 10% of its buses/goods vehicles are ideal due to driver's shortage/absenteeism/driver's illness/employee attrition etc and existing staffs are not showing much interest on overtime work. To address this issue management of AIBS logistics has appointed a private research team. After a detail study of three months, team has recommended the following recommendations to the management.

1. An inward protection conspire for Employees Family Welfare Scheme with commitment from both worker and the employer must be presented which gives a remuneration of Rs. 250000 to the ward of the representative who dies while in service.

2. Medical Reimbursement must be given comparable to government part. Progress for significant disease and individual ailment of the worker and their wards.

3. A Scheme to provide monthly scholarships to children of employees/officers studying in different courses.

4. Revenue incentive scheme:

   a. This scheme is applicable to drivers and conductors.

   b. In Volvo and multi axel services 2.5% of traffic revenue collection.

   c. In other bus services 3% of the traffic revenue collection.

5. Counseling: To propel the work compel for most extreme profitability a guiding plan ought to be embraced in AIBS Logistics. It helps in diminishing non-attendance there by expanding the efficiency, decrease in the mishap rate and change in the conduct of the representatives with the travelers.

6. De-Addiction center:

   a. To avoid liquor manhandle among all representatives as a piece of the responsibility regarding the well being and welfare of its worker.

   b. To educate the workers on the risks and results of liquor manhandle uncommonly in light of a legitimate concern for the suburbanite security and help all representatives to defeat this propensity.

A private research team has also estimated the additional burden of 14.6 crore to implement the above policies. At the same time research team has recommended to generate the additional revenue by displaying the advertisements of other companies/business on AIBS logistics vehicles (buses, goods vehicles, transport vehicles).

The Management of AIBS logistics is reconsidering the recommendations as it is worried about

a. Displaying the advertisements of other companies on its vehicles may harm brand image of the AIBS logistics.

b. AIBS logistics has to set up a separate department to take care of advertisements and its affairs. This is costly affair for the management in terms of additional work force, their salary, infrastructure etc.

c. At the same time AIBS Logistics management is in dilemma to accept all recommendations which will reduce the profit margin of the company.

But before it is too late the Management of AIBS Logistics has to act on the current situation to tackle the near future problems like employee attrition, brand image of the company, profit margin, employee welfare schemes etc.

## Discussions

a. If you are the part of AIBS Logistics management, will you accept all the recommendations of the private research team?

b. What measures do you suggest to AIBS Logistics management to generate additional revenue sources without major capital outlay?

c. "Displaying the advertisements of other companies on its vehicles may harm brand image of the AIBS logistics." What is your opinion on statement?

# PAPER ADVERTISEMENTS

Growing number of Indian population working in multinational companies has given rise to the disposable income of people. The growing income has changed the way people dress, eat, talk, and lead a life. These lifestyle changes have bought many fold changes in the way customer shops, kind of products he/she purchases, where he/she wants to shop. All these changes have given a different look to retail stores.

Retail in India is one of the growing sector in the country, it is projected that retail market will reach US $1.3 trillion by 2020. It is estimated that by 2020, expenditure of Indian consumer will be US $3.60 trillion, as compared to US $1.25 trillion. The growth of Indian retail has increased the participation from foreign and other private players in development of retail market (IBEF, 2017). Following are different retail formats in India, a. Departmental Stores, b. Hypermarkets, c. Supermarkets,/Convenience Stores, d. Specialty Stores, e. Cash & Carry Stores.(IBEF, 2017).

Retail industry caters to product groups like Clothing and Fashion, Consumer Durables, Home Interiors and Furniture, Grocery, Optical, Automobiles, Footwear, Stationery, Kids wear & other kid items, Books, etc.

The Internet industry in India is estimated to reach US $250 billion by 2020, with number of mobile internet users to reach to 650 million and high-speed internet users to touch 550 million. Smartphone and high-speed internet penetration has transformed the way consumers shop now a days (IBEF, 2018). To add to this, customer expectations and growth prospect of retail has intensified the competition in the Indian retail market. Propelled by this, e-retail in India is estimated to touch US $200 billion by 2026 (IBEF, 2018).

For customer convenience, and to meet location specific requirements, retail companies spread their presence across the city. For healthy growth, many retail companies in India have been expanding to Tier-II & Tier III cities (EY & RAI, 2014). Because of this geographical spread, retail companies in India bank on print media for mass coverage (Exchange for Media.com, 2015).

As per TAM AdEx report, in 2014 the composition of advertising by retailers was 4.7% for print, 0.9% for TV and 6.1% for Radio (Exchange for Media.com, 2015).

As per Audit Bureau of Circulations (ABC), in India, print media is flourishing, is on the rise and expanding its presence across the geography in spite of huge competition from other mediums like TV,

Radio and Digital (ABC, 2017). Growth in literacy and urbanization, ease of reading, cost of newspaper and most importantly home delivery are the main reason for growth in newspaper circulations in India (ABC, 2017).

Highlights of Print media as per ABC Report 8-May-2017

|  | 2006 | 2016 | Increase | CAGR |
|---|---|---|---|---|
| Average copies per day | 3.91 cr | 6.28 cr | 2.37 cr | 4.87% |
| No. publishing centers | 659 | 910 | 251 | 3.28% |

Source: Audit Bureau Of Circulations, Press Release, 8-May-2017

CAGR – Compound Annual Growth Rate

From 2006 to 2016, Growth of print media zone wise is as follows –

| Zone | CAGR |
|---|---|
| North | 7.83% |
| South | 4.95% |
| West | 2.81% |
| East | 2.63% |

Source: Audit Bureau of Circulations, Press Release, 8-May-2017

CAGR – Compound Annual Growth Rate

North zone in India is growing at a rate of 7.83%, which is highest as compared to other zones in India. East zone is the least among the four zones of India with CAGR of 2.63%.

From 2006 to 2016, Growth of print media language wise is as follows–

| Language | CAGR |
|---|---|
| Hindi | 8.76% |
| Telugu | 8.28% |
| Kannada | 6.40% |
| Tamil | 5.51% |
| Malayalam | 4.11% |
| English | 2.87% |
| Punjabi | 1.53% |
| Marathi | 1.50% |
| Bengali | 1.49% |

Source: Audit Bureau Of Circulations, Press Release, 8-May-2017

CAGR – Compound Annual Growth Rate

South languages comprising Telugu, Kannada, Tamil, & Malayalam are growing at an average rate of 6.08%. As compared to developed markets, the print industry in India is on growth track. Globally over the last few years, print industry is struggling to find its relevance in the media market, because of digital impact. Now a days, readers prefer the medium which is available 24 × 7 and at their convenience. Though print industry in India also faces the same challenges, but is growing at rate of 7.8 percent from 2011 to 2016 (KPMG India's analysis and estimates 2016–2017).

India is a country with multi-culture and multi-lingual, there is a strong connection with regional language readership. Regional language newspapers not only understand local tastes and preferences of readers, but also have better reach to Tier-II and Tier-III cities. This has acted as a major reason for growth of print media in India, also made advertisers to look for Hindi and other regional languages for advertisements. (KPMG India's analysis and estimates 2016–2017).

Year-on-Year Top 10 (Sector-wise) contributors to newspaper advertisement

| Categories | 2014 | 2015 | 2016 | Change from 2015 |
|---|---|---|---|---|
| FMCG | 13.5% | 14.6% | 15.0% | ▲ |
| Auto | 11.9% | 12.8% | 14.0% | ▲ |
| Education | 9.4% | 9.8% | 10.0% | ▲ |
| Real Estate | 8.0% | 7.0% | 6.0% | ▼ |
| Clothing/Fashion/Jeweler | 6.1% | 6.0% | 5.0% | ▼ |
| E-Commerce | 2.2% | 4.3% | 3.0% | ▼ |
| Telecom/Internet/DTH | 3.7% | 3.8% | 3.0% | ▼ |
| Retail | 5.3% | 5.6% | 5.0% | ▼ |
| BFSI | 4.8% | 4.7% | 5.0% | ▲ |
| HH Durables | 4.2% | 4.6% | 5.0% | ▲ |
| Others | 24.9% | 22.5% | 25.0% | ▲ |

Source: The Pitch Madison Advertising Report, 2017

(KPMG India's analysis and estimates 2016–2017).

| ▲ | Increase | ▼ | Decrease |
|---|---|---|---|

FMCG, Auto, and education sectors contribute to 39% of the print media. There is 0.6% decrease in the newspaper advertisements in retail sector.

Newspaper advertisements play an important role in creating awareness about the product and brand, which in turn might help companies to boost the sales. Advertisements in general have some psychological impact on consumer and create some perception about the company, product, and brand (Mohit Bansal and Shubham Gupta, 2014).

Perception and attitude towards a product and brands are important aspects found to affect the consumer behavior. In the dynamic informative world, consumers are filled with too much of information about companies, products, and brands. Information content of advertisements has major impact on consumer behavior. (Mohit Bansal and Shubham Gupta, 2014).

Considering the nature of retail business, many retailers employ different marketing strategies to influence consumer-buying behavior, one of such strategy is the newspaper advertisements. Evaluate print ad strategies adopted by retail companies and impact of these advertisements on consumer buying behavior.

## Refer Annexure:1 for Detail Advertisements

Paper Ad No-1, Times of India, Dated – 20-Jan-2018

Paper Ad No-2, Times of India, Dated – 20-Jan-2018

Paper Ad No-3, Times of India, Dated – 24-Jan-2018

Paper Ad No-4.a, Times of India, Dated – 26-Jan-2018

Paper Ad No-4.b, Times of India, Dated – 26-Jan-2018

Paper Ad No-4.c, Times of India, Dated – 26-Jan-2018

Paper Ad No-4.d, Times of India, Dated – 26-Jan-2018

Paper Ad No-4.e, Times of India, Dated – 26-Jan-2018

Paper Ad No-4.f, Times of India, Dated – 26-Jan-2018

Paper Ad No-5, Times of India, Dated – 10-Feb-2018

# UNCERTAINTY IN DECISION MAKING AT SHREE CHAKRA TYRES

The board of directors of Shree chakra tyre manufacturing company is planning future production capacity requirements for its particular tractor tyre considering one of the four demand rates as low(D1), Normal(D2), medium (D3) and high(D4) is possible.

The corresponding production plant capacity to match each of the demand rates has already been calculated to be respectively small (W), normal(X), medium(Y), and large plant (Z). In the below table present value terms the estimated total profits associated with each alternative capacity levels are given, assuming that each growth rate in turn occurred with certainty.

| Production capacity level | Demand rate | | | |
|---|---|---|---|---|
| | D1 | D2 | D3 | D4 |
| W | 26 | 47 | 68 | 78 |
| X | 23 | 51 | 77 | 87 |
| Y | 18 | 55 | 86 | 96 |
| Z | 17 | 31 | 47 | 57 |

The board of directors of Shree chakra tyre manufacturing company is faced with problems of uncertainty in taking decision as large scale commitments of company resources are involved. Their fore Board is considering to carrying out market survey to get a clear understanding of the market and decision variables.

Based on the market survey the conditional probability matrix of four possible out comes which are defined as P,Q,R and S indicating occurrence of demand rate D1,D2,D3 and D4 are shown in the below table.

| Survey result | Demand Rate | | | |
|---|---|---|---|---|
| | D1 | D2 | D3 | D4 |
| P | 0.70 | 0.07 | 0.15 | 0.08 |
| Q | 0.07 | 0.13 | 0.40 | 0.40 |

*Contd.*

| Survey result | Demand Rate | | | |
|---|---|---|---|---|
| | D1 | D2 | D3 | D4 |
| R | 0.03 | 0.3 | 0.40 | 0.27 |
| S | 0.2 | 0.5 | 0.05 | 0.25 |

Based on the forecast and assessments of all those facts likely to influence the future demand of the product, the subjective probability of demand growth rate D1, D2, D3 and D4 are 0.20, 0.10, 0.35, and 0.35 respectively.

## Discussions

a. You as a strategic consultant of the company which alternative production capacity should be suggested?

b. Will you suggest market survey? If yes how decision process is affected by market survey.

# CUSTOMER MIGRATION AT ABC CARGO

ABC Cargo Company is a new late entrant in the cargo business is bleeding due to high customer migration caused by alternative promotional schemes run by the rivals. There are four private cargo service providers. In the highly competitive environment, it is natural that almost everybody is switching service providers. But while gaining a new customer is good news for any service providers, the flip side it is a loss of customers for other service providers.

All most every industry is affected by customer migration phenomenon. It happens due to discounts, offers, service quality, value added service etc.

According to research conducted by ABC Cargo Company, the cost of acquiring new customer is more than five times that of retaining an existing customer. So when calculated the 1 percent of customer migration per month, ABC Cargo Company is losing 12 percent of its customer every year.

As a fight for customer ownership intensifies Cargo service providers will have to compete heavily to win existing customer of competitors as well as to retain their existing customer. The policies to counter this migration problem will depend on:

a.  Adopting new market strategies to retain customers

b.  Offering value added services to customers and minimize the customer migration.

c.  Retaining existing customers with discounts, offers and customer satisfaction process.

The data of customer migration is shown for the Cargo service providers in below table:

| Service provider | Migration Rate (percent) | Retention Rate (percent) |
|---|---|---|
| X Cargo | 12.0 | 88.0 |
| Y Cargo | 18.5 | 81.5 |
| Z Cargo | 10.5 | 89.5 |
| ABC Cargo | 12.0 | 88.0 |

ABC Cargo has a customer base of 8.18 lakh with a market share of 10.4 percent in the Cargo business. At a migration rate of 2.5 – 5 percent per month for the Cargo industry, ABC Cargo is losing

2750 customers every month as a result of customer migration. Their fore it is very important for ABC Cargo Company to put proper solution in place to overcome this situation.

The following data shows the customer base in Cargo industry.

| Service provider | Customer Base (in Lakh) | Market Share (percent) |
|---|---|---|
| X Cargo | 19.5 | 24.78 |
| Y Cargo | 26.8 | 34.06 |
| Z Cargo | 24.2 | 30.75 |
| ABC Cargo | 8.18 | 10.4 |

Suggest the solution that should enable the ABC Cargo Company to gain better decision variables that influence customer migration. It should also enable the company understand which category of customer are likely migrating and why? This will help the company to take necessary steps to overcome the customer migration problem.

# CASES ON FINANCIAL MANAGEMENT

# INVESTMENT PLAN FOR SENIOR CITIZENS

Dr. Shrinidhi is considered as famous Doctor in Bangalore, retired at the age of 58 after 30 years of service. Dr. Shrinidhi has two adult children who are also practicing doctors. At the time of his retirement, Dr. Shrinidhi owned a bungalow at Bangalore and Gulbarga. He had savings of Rs. 5,00,000 in bank deposits and owned shares and bonds of repute companies. Dr. Shrinidhi sold the 25 years old securities through a share purchase plan at the time of retirement. The sale proceeds were Rs. 17,00,000 after taxes. To run happy and healthy life after retirement, Dr. Shrinidhi requires pre-tax income of Rs. 400000 – Rs. 500000.

Dr. Shrinidhi is in need of consultancy with respect to manage his portfolio. The following table gives different securities available in the market. Three portfolios have been constructed.

| Type of security | Yield* | Portfolio | | |
|---|---|---|---|---|
| | | A | B | C |
| Short-Term Commercial Bank Deposit | 10% | 2,00,000 | – | 2,00,000 |
| Tax-free bonds of PSU | 11.5% | – | 4,00,000 | 2,00,000 |
| Long-term Debentures of | | | | |
| AAA Rated | 13% | – | – | 10,00,000 |
| AA Rated | 13.5% | – | 10,00,000 | – |
| Local Bonds | 8% | 16,00,000 | 4,00,000 | – |
| Preference shares | 12% | – | – | 4,00,000 |
| Equity shares of IT Companies | 20% | 2,00,000 | 6,00,000 | 4,00,000 |
| Equity shares of Banking Companies | 17% | 2,00,000 | 4,00,000 | – |
| Equity shares | 16.5% | 22,00,000 | 16,00,000 | 22,00,000 |
| | | 44,00,000 | 44,00,000 | 44,00,000 |

*Assumed current yield

## Discussions

1. Suggest the best portfolio mix.

2. Give alternative plans for investments

3. Is investment in bonds based on the ratings advisable?

# STOCK MARKET CRASH – KHETAN PAREKH (KP)

Ketan Parekh (KP) was a noted Bull and known for his investment strategies. He worked as stock broker in Mumbai (India). He was found guilty because of his involvement in share market manipulations in the late 90s and in the year 2000. He was sentenced to two years imprisonment by CBI in 2014. It was learnt that, KP was trained in Harshad Mehta owned Grow More Investments Mumbai. KP used to buy more shares in small companies and influenced with his different strategies like circular trading to boost the prices.

On March 1st 2001 the sudden crash shook the entire stock market and economy. This made Securities and Exchange Board of India – SEBI to order for immediate investigation for crises of the stock market. The investigation team was asked to check the books of suspected brokers. The central bank RBI has instructed the banks involved in it to submit the information related to their capital market exposure. The media coverage with respect to private banks involved in it has made RBI to take immediate action to probe on it. The Bombay Stock Exchange President Mr. AnandRathi has put up his papers for the president post as he was alleged that, he had used some privileged information which contributed to the crash. The fear of this incident has badly effected on stock market. By end of March, 2001, it was reported that at least 8 people committed suicide and more than 100 investors went bankrupted.

The major points discussed in the whole scam about funding capital market operation and lending funds against collateral security, validity of dual control of co-operative banks. According to sources, these cooperative banks' transactions were inspected on the doubt of funding capital market operations and leading funds against collateral security. Few Analysts pointed out about, RBI's inspection of bank accounts once n two years. One of the major crashes was happened in stock market after the arrest of noted bull Mr. Khetan Parekh on 30th March, 2001 for defrauding Bank of India of about $300 lakh.

## KP Wealth

KhetanParekhs (known as KP) has good link with many business people and investors across world. Australian media king Kerry Packer has partnered KP with $250 million venture capital fund. KP's network has extended everywhere. He has become the best broker within a short span of time. There was huge demand for ICE (Information, Communications and Entertainment) companies and accordingly their shares prices have been raised early in 1999 across the world. KPs' favorite stocks include through his Triumph International company are Amitabh Bachan Corpration Limited (ABCL), Mukta Arts, Tipsand Pritish Nandy Commn., HFCL, Global Telesystems (Global), Zee Telefilms, Crest Communications, and PentaMedia Graphics. His strong research team keeps the track of the market and based on the analysis, the team has selected these companies. These companies are having high growth with small capital base. KP could take the advantage of low liquidity. His companies are popularly known as 'KP-10' stock.

Triumph International Company held stock during July, 1999 around 1.2 million shares with 16% stake of Global Telesystems, 25% stake in Aftek Infosys and 15% in Zee Telefilms and HFCL. There was a marginal increase in stock market from January to July 1999. So there was 57% hike in the shares price of HFCL and Global Tlesystems by 200%. This made many investors, brokers and fund managers to invest heavily in KP-10 Stocks. Accordingly they made huge amount of money. Due heavy investment by many investors including institutional investors, KP-10 stocks were featured as top trades stocks in the market by January 2000. With this, KP was struggling to manage the huge funds and became difficult to control.

## Reasons for Success of KP Stocks

KP was treated as one of the intelligent financial managers and brokers. His heavy investment in different companies would have cost him around Rs. 800 million in July 1999. He had borrowed money from Banks and financial institutes and companies like HFCL etc. He used very simple and fairly strategy. He bought shares when they were trading at low prices and observed the prices till it goes up while continuously trading. He pledged the shares when the price was high, with banks as collateral for funds. Ahmadabad based bank, Madhavapura Mercantile Cooperative Bank (MMCB) was KP's main ally in the scam. Due to continuous and large investment, KP's hands were empty without cash and faced liquidity problem during December, 2000. KP sought the help of Banks for meeting his liquidity requirements and accordingly he has approached Madhavapura Mercantile Cooperative Bank (MMCB).

KP was very intelligent not only in managing finance; he knew different techniques for raising money from banks. KP used MMCB in two different ways. 1. Pay Order 2. Loan from MMCB at Madvi Mumbai.

In the first case, KP issued cheques drawn on Bank of India to MMCB for which MMCB issued pay orders without considering any collateral securities. MMCB crossed its capital market exposure in this regard according to sources. KP discounted the pay orders at Bank of India. It was noticed during inspection of RBI team that, out of Rs. 10 billion loan issued by MMCB to stock market, KP and team has been given Rs. 8 billion.

In the second case, KP's companies and his associates borrowed heavy money from Madhavapura Mercantile Cooperative Bank (MMCB) from Madvi branch using 16 accounts directly and brokers firms. It was also alleged that, few brokers and Mr. Vinit Parikh the owner of Madhur Capital and son of MMCB Chairman Mr. Ramesh Parikh also acted on KP behalf to borrow money. KP used to get loan by keeping shares as collateral securities.

KP used his accounts held in Bank of India to discount 248 pay orders worth Rs. 24 billion from January to March 2001. Many banks like SBI, BOI, PNB etc. were facing problems with respect to MMCB pay orders. Such banks have lost huge amounts in this regard. The name of Global Trust Bank (GTB) was heard many times in this scam. GTB has given fund to KP by crossing the prescribed limit.

KP and his associates held around 10% stake in this bank. According media reports, KP with the help of former CMD of GTB Mr. Ramesh Gelli played with stock price of GTB to their favorable before its merger with UTI.

The market started tumbling in March 2000 due to fall in NASDAQ, accordingly the price of KP's stock have been declined. This was badly affected to KP's business. Many banks insisted KP to refund the loan or to give more collateral security. Institutional investor like Mutual fund, insurance and may more have started reducing their exposure in KP-10 shares in April 2000. The stock market continued declining. The Sensex has fallen down by 23%, NASDAQ by 35% and KP-10 stocks have declined by 67%. From May, 2000 onwards, the improvement was seen in the market globally and locally. There was a favorable seen for KP-10 stocks. HFCL has risen almost doubled from Rs. 790 to 1353 Global Company's share price reached to Rs. 1153 and after Infosys reached to Rs. 1000. however the NASDAQ crashed again and technology based share prices were badly affected. This had also hit the Indian market. Many investors withdrew their stake in the companies. KP has lost money due to this and started facing financial crunch. Since there was fall in the market and KP-10 stocks, many investors rushed to withdrew their shares, this hit the payment problem of stock exchanges including Calcutta Stock Exchange (CSE). The Calcutta Stock Exchange faced problems like, illegal and badla business. SCE being the third bigger in terms of volumes of shares traded, it had helped KP to cover his operations from his rivals in Mumbai.

At the behest of KP, brokers used to buy shares at CSE. Though the shares were in the name of brokers but KP used to hold them to cover the any losses happened due to fall in the price and paid 2.5% interest on weekly basis to the brokers. The shares held by brokers of KP at CSE reduced to Rs. 7 billion from Rs. 12 billion by February, 2001. Further KP's badla payment around Rs. 6 billion were not honored on time for the settlement. About 70 brokers including Dinesh Singhania, Sanjay Khemani and Ashok Podar defaulted on their payments. The values of stock held by brokers of SCE have fallen down to Rs. 3 billion which made brokers to insist KP for the payment. By this time it was inevitable to KP to approach and get loan from MMCB. MMCB's loan without collateral security (earlier loans were having collateral securities) to KP has substantially been increased from January, 2001.

Securities and Exchange Board of India (SEBI) has introduced many changes to control market like reducing additional volatility margin from 80% to 60%, restrictions on short sales, suspension brokermember directors of BSE's governing board, banning trading of president vice presidents treasurers of stock exchanges, and badla system. SEBI also introduced a rolling settlement system.

Court released KP on bail in May 2001. The whole scam shook the nation and its economy. Thousands of investors lost their money. Few committed suicide. Some of the investors stopped trading in the market. It was opined that, more than a fraud, KP was an example within the Indian financial and regulatory systems. Market regulator could have controlled the damage of at least Rs. 2000 billion. The brokers, bankers, promoters, were the reasons for scams. The actions of SEBI were widely criticized. Few analysts also felt that SEBI's market intelligence was poor in handling it. There was media report comment, which says that KP's arrest was also not due to the SEBI's timely action but the result of complaints by Bank of India. SEBI should have acted when market was fluctuating. It ignored the large positions built up by some operators. Many exchanges were not happy with the decision of banning the badla system without alternative arrangement as they felt it would rig the liquidity in the market.

## Discussions

1. Understand and comment the regulatory framework of SEBI involved in handling the case.

2. What went wrong with Ketan Parekh?

3. Do you think, this was an example of weak regulatory system in India? Discuss the statement to justify your stand with valid reasons.

4. Compare Indian regulatory system with any one of the foreign regulator system. List out strengths and weakness of both the systems.

## Reference

1. www.wikipedia.org/w/index.php?title=Ketan_Parekh

2. http://indiansharemarketinfotips.blogspot.in

3. www.nseindia.com

4. www.bseindia.com

5. SEBI Guidelines and information

6. Business world magazine

# BANKER'S DECISION ON LOAN

In recent past, it is seen that most of the banks are having young managers with age 25 to 30 and above. Mr. Hari, a branch manager of a commercial bank is young talent from Mangalore transferred to Hubli. The new place is small banking area with limited transactions which is new area and new experience to him.

Mr. Hari was insisted by his boss for the business enhancement from the date of his joining as branch manager. He has taken it as a challenge and used different strategies for meeting the requirements of his Boss. He has used different strategies like telecalling, meeting new customers and convincing and highlighting them about importance of deposits etc. he has also started visiting new and unbanked areas. He met business leaders, professionals, institutions for the new corporate accounts. Hubli being commercial hub for north Karnataka, his banks have many tough competitor Banks and Financial Institutes. With aggressive marketing strategies which he learnt from his MBA degree has yielded positive result in the initial stage. He has increased the number of transactions with his team. The owner of Laxmi Apartments came forward to open deposit account in the Bank with Rs. 20 lakh. Meanwhile the manager has taken approval from his head office to sanction a mortgage loan Rs. 30 lakh to Laxmi Apartment owner.

After few days, the manager Mr. Hari was called by his Boss for the discussion about his work. Mr. Hari was excited and eager to greet and meet the team in the head quarter thinking that, his work is being appreciated. But the decision of the Boss was something different. Boss was annoyed with the work of Mr. Hari. He pointed out a mistake done by manager. There was a serious mistake happened in the bank's deposit operations center in previous month. The cheque worth Rupees One lakh deposited into Laxmi Apartments' rental collection account two months ago were returned to the bank for non-availability of funds. However Bank could not deduct the charges for bad cheques from Laxmi Apartment Account and nor returned the cheque to the party but the cheque was placed by clerk in his bottom desk drawer and forgot about it.

The auditor located the cheque during the audit process of the Bank, The manager was objected and asked to debit the charges to Lakshmi Apartment account and return the cheque to the party. The manager argues to his boss that this action may not be right, because, as per the bank's written policy, cheques accepted for deposit cannot be returned after the tenth business day following their date of deposit. In addition, Mr. Hari explains that, one of the conditions of the bank's mortgage loan approval to Lakshmi Apartment is that the owner should maintain a major deposit account with his branch. He knows that if he charges the Lakshmi Apartment account for the bad cheque loss, he will anger Lakshmi Apartment, lose the 20 lakh deposit accounts and the new mortgage loan, and sacrifice all future business from Lakshmi Apartment to competing financial institutions in his own market. Mr. Hari's boss claims that he understands his dilemma, but he is adamant in his instruction to him. The bank cannot afford Rs. 20 lakh loss to a new corporate depositor, and he must debit Lakshmi Apartment account to cover the bad cheque loss. And also, Mr. Hari is calmly warned that discussing this matter with any other senior officers of the bank will prove most damaging to his career.

## Discussions

1. What should manager do?

2. Is Boss's decision correct?

3. Discuss the consequences of decision with respect to business.

4. Do you recommend the appointment of young managers to banking sector?

# EMPLOYEES' ATTRITION AND CHANGE OF JOB

The employees attrition rate* in the recent past is increasing continuously. It happens mainly in sales department. Youngsters are not sticking to one job for a long period. In this connection Ms. Shrujani received a mail from Bangalore based company in the late evening with respect to an important interview scheduled for the very next day at 10.30 am. Due to Ms. Shrujani's request the earlier interview was already postponed once by the same company. The mail categorically states that no postponement of the date or the time would be possible. Being the second and important interview, she can't miss it.

There are a number of trains between Bangalore and Hubli (where Shrujani is now). There are regular private and government buses and even shared taxis are available. Hubli being commercial city has flight facility in the morning to Bangalore.

| Mode of transport | From Hubli | To Bangalore | Fare | Remarks |
|---|---|---|---|---|
| **Flight** | 8.30 am | 10.00 am | Rs. 5000 | Seats available |
| **Govt. and Private Buses (sleeper, semi sleeper and general)**<br>(7 to 8 Hours journey)<br>Frequency at every hour from 7 pm to 10 pm and at every half an hour from 10 pm to 11.30 pm. No buses from mid night to early morning. | | | Rs. 400 to 800 | Seats available |
| **Train–1**   (8 Hours journey) | 10.30 pm | 6.30 am | Rs. 200 to Rs. 1500 | Seats available in A/C and SC |
| **Train–2**   (6 Hours journey) | 1.00 am | 7.00am | Rs. 200 to Rs. 1500 | Seats likely to be available in SC only. |
| **Intercity Train**   (5 Hours journey) | 5.00 am | 10.00am | Rs. 200 to Rs. 1500 | Seats may be available |
| **Shared Taxis** (6 Hours journey)<br>Taxi starts with 4 passengers only. No taxis from mid night to 3.00 am early morning. | | | Rs. 500 per passenger | |

*Employees/attrition rate = number of attritions/average number of employees x 100

Since the mail received by the candidate is in the late evening, she does not have time for preparation for the interview. And not having enough time to collect more relevant data also. She does not have close relatives to stay in Bangalore.

## Discussions

1. Suggest and Implement the best decision

2. Discuss on the employees attritions.

## Challenges

- Reaching the destination in time in comfortable zone.

- Road block and traffic in Hubli and Bangalore.

- Booking tickets.

- Food.

- Packing.

- Preparation for the interview.

- Availability of clothes, money Etc.

# CAPITAL BUDGETING

## Capital Budgeting (I)

Hindustan Co. Ltd Delhi is known for its quality products. Due to its increasing demand towards its products, company is thinking of expanding its business by adding a new products line to supplement its existing Line. It is proposed that, the new product line will involve cash investments of Rs. 1 crore. A cash inflow of Rs. 12,50,000 is expected in 1ˢᵗ year and Rs. 5,50,000 is expected to increase in every subsequent year till 5 years.

## Discussions

1. Assuming the required rate of return is 14%, determine the NPV of the project.

2. Analyze the consequence of acceptance of proposal

3. Analyze the NPV with required rate of return of 11%

4. Company needs to know the rate at which its investment is going to recover and asked your suggestion.

## Capital Budgeting (II)

Renuka Sugars Ltd. is one of the listed companies in sugars industry. Due to increasing demand for its product in the market, there was proposal from marketing department to expand its capacity. Production department has asked finance department to analyze the following proposals.

Proposal-I have the initial investment cost of Rs. 20 lakh and Proposal-II has Rs. 56 lakh. Both the proposals will yield the income at the end next five years. Assume discount rate of return is 12%

| Year End | Proposal-I | Proposal-II |
|----------|------------|-------------|
| 1 | 6,60,000 | 18,00,000 |
| 2 | 10,00,000 | 22,00,000 |
| 3 | 7,40,000 | 24,00,000 |
| 4 | 6,00,000 | 16,00,000 |
| 5 | 4,00,000 | 14,00,000 |

## Discussions

1. Analyze the proposals with your supporting calculations and suggest which proposal is recommended to choose.

2. Suggest the rate of return at which the initial investment can be recovered.

3. What is the period of recovery of investment?

4. Understand the expansion strategies of Renuka Sugars across the world.

# Capital Budgeting (III)

Following are the two mutually exclusive projects given for the analysis.

| Particulars | Project A | Project B |
|---|---|---|
| Investment | 2,00,000 | 3,00,000 |
| Life in years | 4 | 7 |
| Cash inflows pa. | 75,000 | 80,000 |
| Scrap value | 25,000 | 15,000 |
| Annuity factor | 2.8550 | 4.1604 |
| Discounting factor | 0.5718 | 0.3759 |

# Discussions

Find which of the project is recommended and why. Assuming no taxes and cost of capital is at 15%.

# LEASING VS BUYING-BORROWING

Toys making industry is one of the booming industries in the present scenario. It is seen that, China and some other countries have entered into Indian market and selling their products at low price. With low price being charged by China based companies, Indian small scale industries including toys manufacturing companies are suffering huge amount of loss. Though the government is levying anti dumping duty on certain items, but the china products have captured the Indian market. And even most of the online companies are selling china based products only.

Veda Co. Ltd. is known for making kids toys of different ranges in India. Presently, it has one manufacturing plant in Mysore having production capacity of 15 lakh toys annually. The toys are being sold through registered dealers in India.

Due to quality and innovative products, the company is getting more orders from different locations. The Marketing Head Mr. Anjan has submitted a proposal to the managing director and CEO of the company to expand the production capacity to 20 lakh. Accordingly the MD has accepted the proposal and asked the production department head to consider the same. The Production head says, presently company does not have required equipments to increase the capacity. The company decides to purchase a new machine and collects the quotations. As per quotation, one manufacturer is ready to supply the machinery for Rs. 62.5 crore with five years life and no salvage.

Lease financing is the booming sector in India. Most of the companies are going for hiring machineries on lease bases instead of investing huge amount of money. The company has two alternative thought in this regard now. Company can buy the equipment and be financed by borrowing from the commercial bank at 10% interest per annum. And the equipment can be alternatively taken on lease from the leasing company at Rs. 17.5 crore annual lease rentals. The leasing company would bear the taxes, insurance and maintenance expenses Rs. 3 crore annually. Assume straight line deprecation for tax purpose. Company is in the 30% tax bracket.

## Discussions

a. Advise the company on the choice of alternatives of leasing and acquisition of equipment.

b. What is your opinion on foreign companies selling their products at low price in India.

# DECISION ON CHOOSING THE SHARES

Automobile industry is one of the booming sectors in India with Indian and foreign brands. Number of people owning two wheelers and four wheelers is increasing continuously. As per the data provided by statista.com the number of two-wheeler (scooters, motorcycles and mopeds) vehicles in 2010–11 were 1,17,68,910 which is increased to 1,59,75,561 in 2014–15. There is drastic change in the year 2016–17 and increased by 10% to reach 1,75,89,511.

The following table gives the information of Indian two wheelers companies Bajaj Auto and TVS Motors ltd.

| Particulars | Bajaj Auto Ltd. | TVS Motors |
|---|---|---|
| Sales revenue in Rs. Crores | 8732.75 | 2597 |
| Net Profit in Rs. Crores | 972.5 | 168.5 |
| Equity in Rs. Crores | 298.5 | 58.5 |
| Book Value | 177.4 | 80.1 |
| EPS | 32.6 | 29.2 |
| Dividend | 80 | 50 |
| Share price as on 06.02.2018 (Rs.) | 3135 | 650 |
| Sectoral Index P/E | 41.49 | 41.49 |
| P/E | 24.47 | 56.81 |
| 52 week High price Rs. | 3139 | 651 |
| 52 week Low price Rs. | 2694 (07 July, 2017) | 390 (06 Feb. 2017) |

*Source: www.nseindia.com*

## Discussions

- Advice the investors on selecting the company for investment purpose?

- Suggest suitable reasons for choosing the scripts.

- Analyze the future growth of automobile sector in India.

## Reference

a. www.statista.com/statistics/318023/two-wheeler-sales-in-india

b. www.nseindia.com

# INSTALLATION OF COFFEE VENDING MACHINE

Pradyumna Investments Ltd. is into stock market operations for last 5 years in Bangalore. It has 50 employees and many clients who are frequent visitors to the office (average number of visitors in a day is 200). The office is situated in MG Road Bangalore. The company provides Tea/Coffee facility to all its employees (twice in a day) and selected visitors (once in a day). It is observed that, around 100 people are served tea and remaining is given coffee. Since the company does not have its own cafeteria nor tea preparation machines; it is getting disturbed in providing tea to its employees and also to the visitors during their visit. The details of expenses are as under.

## 1. Existing System

| # | Particulars | Cost Rs. |
|---|---|---|
| 1 | Cost per cup of Tea | Rs. 5 |
| 2 | Cost per cup of Coffee | Rs. 10 |
| 3 | Labor Charges | Rs. 1000 pm |
| 4 | Maintenance etc. | Rs. 200 pm |
| 6 | Cost of Cups, Saucers, Flask etc. | Rs. 1000 pa |

The finance manager of the company proposed the alternative solution for the above and requested the higher authority with following points.

Since, the company is facing problem in providing the service on time to its employees and visitors, the company may install the Tea/Coffee vending machine in the office to meet the requirements.

If company uses existing cups, cost will be Rs. 1000 pa for maintenance and others. Assume 25 working days in a month. 200 people (including staff and visitors) will take Tea/Coffee on all the working days. The company uses Fixed Installment Method of Depreciation. Cost of capital is 10%.

Details are shown as under.

| # | Details | Cost Rs. |
|---|---------|----------|
| 1 | Cost of the machine | 1,00,000 |
| 2 | Salvage value | Nil |
| 3 | Life of asset | 5 years |
| 4 | Annual maintenance cost | 30,000 |
| 5 | Spare parts etc. | 5,000 |
| 6 | Electricity Charges | Rs. 500 pm |
| 7 | Coffee beans cost per packet (need two packet daily) | Rs. 30 |
| 8 | Tea powder cost per packet (need two packet daily) | Rs. 20 |
| 9 | Cost per Plastic cup | Rs. 0.25 |
| 10 | Milk per liter (need 10 liters daily) | Rs. 40 |
| 11 | Sugar per kg (need 2 kg daily) | Rs. 40 |
| 12 | Labor charges | Rs. 1,000 pm |
| 13 | Water charges | Rs. 500 pm |

# Discussions

a.  As a financial advisor, what would be your opinion on the above

b.  Suggest the best solution with proper reasons and show calculations wherever required.

c.  Suggest any other mode of service if your advice is different from the above two alternatives.

# CASES ON HUMAN RESOURCE MANAGEMENT

# BANGALORE RETAIL

As per USDA Foreign Agricultural Service, GAIN Report (2015), the population of Bangalore was 6.5 million in 2001, and it has grown to 9.6 million by 2011, which is 47 percent growth in the population. Bangalore is considered as most modern cities in India because 90 percent of the population lives in urban areas of the Bangalore district. GDP of the Bangalore city is on the growth path, which is growing at a rate of 8.1 percent from 2007 to 2012. This growing economic factors have made many skilled work force to look towards Bangalore for employment.

## RN Supermarket

RN Food Retail Company has total 100 supermarkets across India.

Average size of store ranges from 1000 to 6500 sq.ft and has following assortment–

a. Fruits & Vegetables

b. Staples

c. Home Needs

d. Food & Beverages

e. Home care

f. Personal care

Company has well qualified HR team in place to manage Human Resources of the company. 'Employee first' is the mantra of the company and devised its strategies around people. The RN Food Retail Company is the first choice of employees. Being in retail sector, company has major human resource challenges in store staffs' compensation, attendance management, working hours and attrition. Company has flat organisation structure for all the departments.

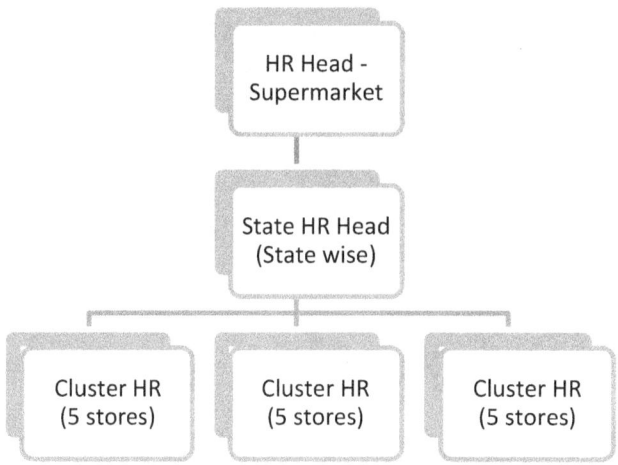

**Chart No. 01:** Organization chart

In a span of a year, company opened 25 supermarkets across Bangalore. Average manpower-budget per store stands at 25 including one Store Manager and two supervisors.

**Table No. 1:** Store-wise Manpower Budget basis Sales

| Store | Sales per month (In lacs) | SM | Supervisor | Customer Service Staff |
|-------|---------------------------|-----|------------|------------------------|
| Store-1 | 0.25 | 1 | 2 | 12 |
| Store-2 | 0.28 | 1 | 2 | 15 |
| Store-3 | 0.32 | 1 | 2 | 18 |
| Store-4 | 0.35 | 1 | 2 | 18 |
| Store-5 | 0.45 | 1 | 3 | 22 |
| Store-6 | 0.38 | 1 | 2 | 18 |
| Store-7 | 0.42 | 1 | 3 | 22 |
| Store-8 | 0.55 | 1 | 3 | 25 |
| Store-9 | 0.60 | 1 | 3 | 25 |
| Store-10 | 0.34 | 1 | 2 | 18 |
| Store-11 | 0.78 | 1 | 3 | 25 |
| Store-12 | 0.90 | 1 | 4 | 25 |
| Store-13 | 0.25 | 1 | 2 | 12 |
| Store-14 | 0.35 | 1 | 2 | 18 |
| Store-15 | 0.36 | 1 | 2 | 18 |
| Store-16 | 0.28 | 1 | 2 | 15 |
| Store-17 | 0.45 | 1 | 3 | 22 |
| Store-18 | 0.55 | 1 | 3 | 25 |
| Store-20 | 0.85 | 1 | 4 | 25 |

| Store | Sales per month (In lacs) | SM | Supervisor | Customer Service Staff |
|---|---|---|---|---|
| Store-21 | 0.35 | 1 | 2 | 18 |
| Store-22 | 0.27 | 1 | 2 | 15 |
| Store-23 | 1.28 | 1 | 6 | 30 |
| Store-24 | 0.50 | 1 | 3 | 25 |
| Store-25 | 0.75 | 1 | 3 | 25 |
| Store-19 | 1.05 | 1 | 6 | 30 |
| | **12.91** | **25** | **71** | **521** |

Education qualification, and average experience of employees varies from designation to designation.

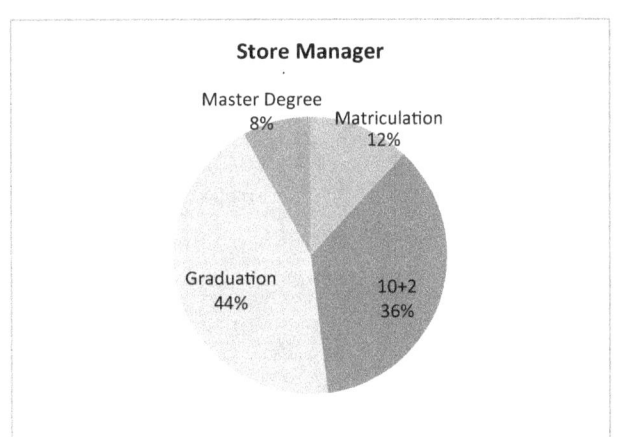
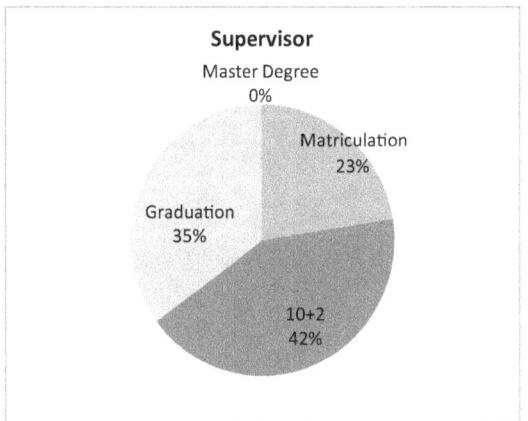
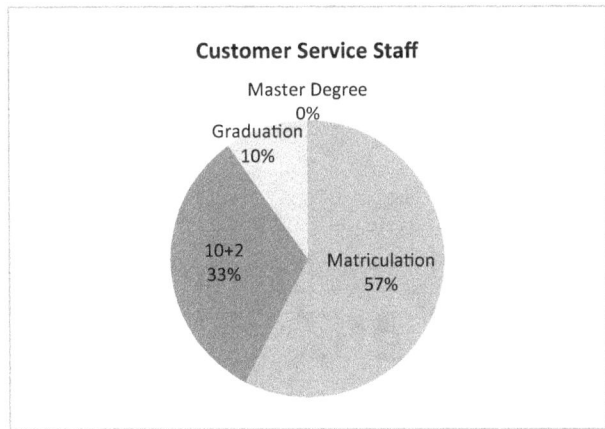

**Graph No. 1, 2, 3, & 4:** Qualification & Experience of employees – Designation-wise.

Gender plays a vital role in retail industry considering the activities and other factors like working hours and travelling convenience. Activities of store staffs include, unloading stocks, counting of stocks, displaying of products, refilling products, cleaning the racks & products, attending customers, billing and home delivery, etc.

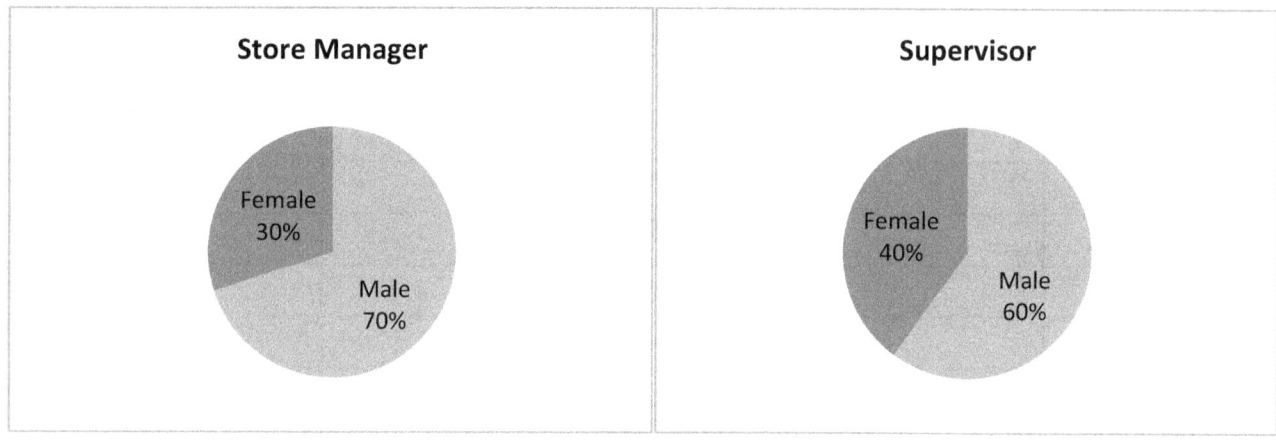

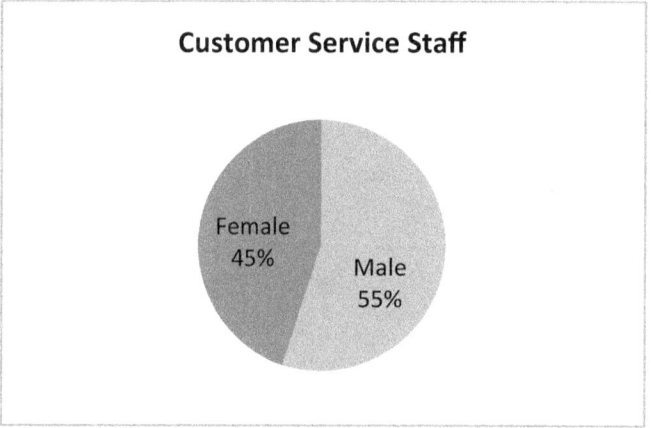

**Graph No. 5, 6, 7:** Gender ratio of employees – Designation-wise.

Bangalore has witnessed huge growth in all sectors including retail. Number of national & international stores has been on the rise. Growing market has created young consumers with high disposable income. This growth has both positive and negative impact on different sectors. In case of retail, the competition has increased because of increasing retail outlets, created job opportunities leading to imbalance in demand & supply of talent.

Employee of retail has many opportunities to choose basis his/her qualification, experience, salary, and preference for profile of the role. This led to huge talent exits in RN Food Retail stores also.

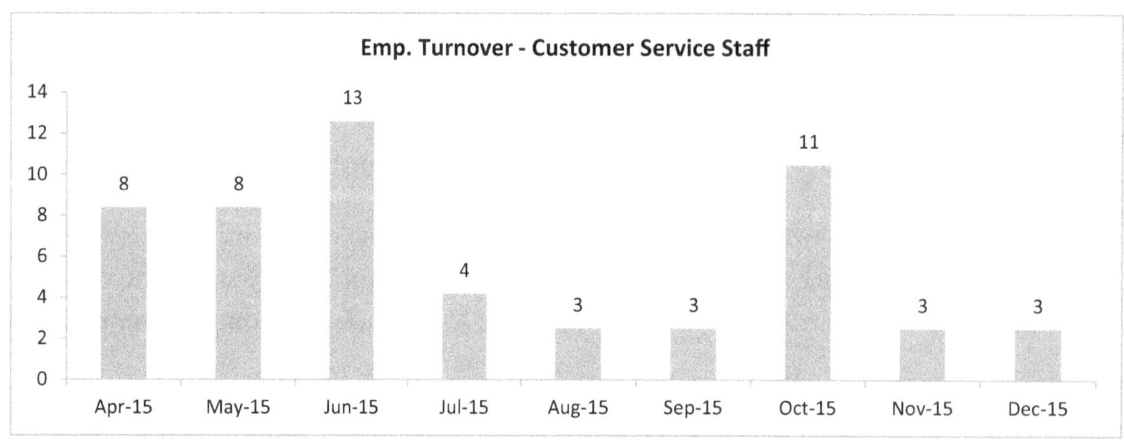

**Graph No. 8:** Employee Turnover – Customer Service Staffs

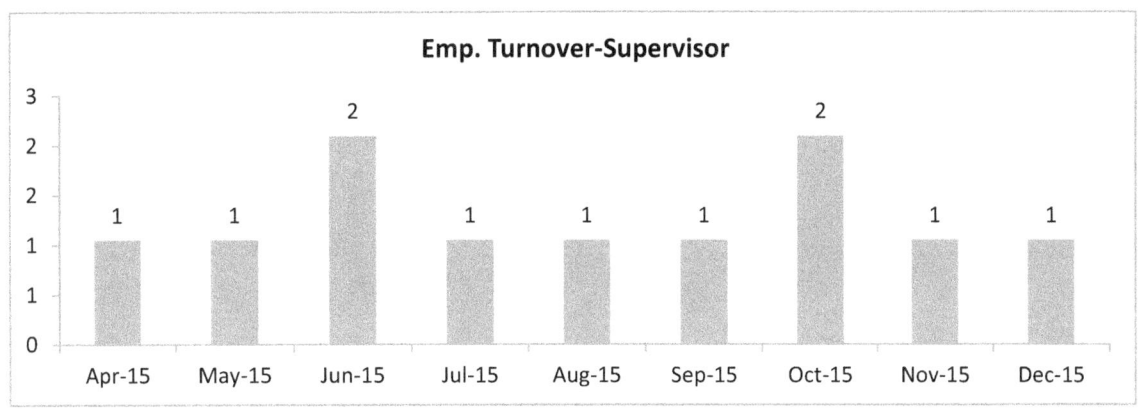

**Graph No. 9:** Employee Turnover – Supervisor

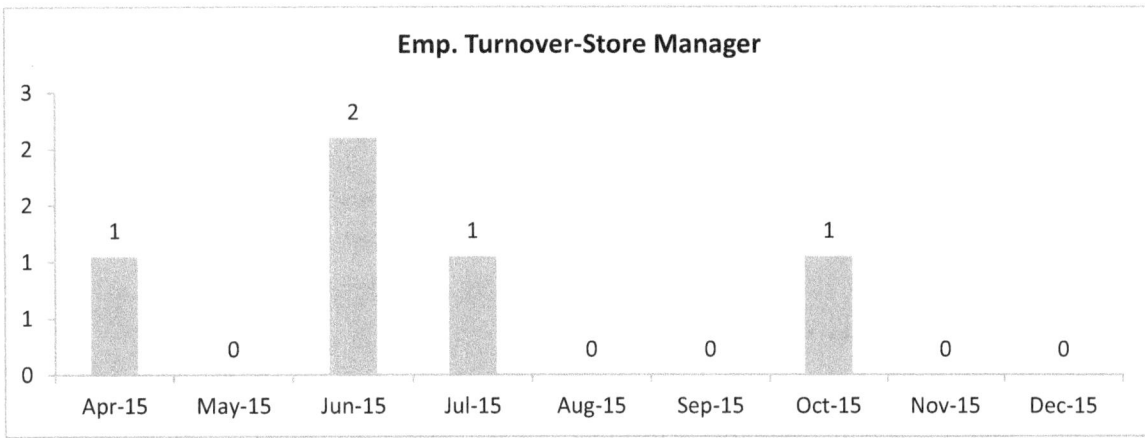

**Graph No. 10:** Employee Turnover – Store Manager

In the recently concluded board meeting, top management of RN Food Retail Company expressed its concern about growing employee turnover. Company also mentioned that, Bangalore is growing market and offers huge opportunity for organized retail. HR department of the company has been asked to prepare action plan around recruitment strategy, induction & orientation, employee handholding, employee engagement, leave policy, attendance & working hours, compensation and leadership skills of store management team.

# PANEL INTERVIEW

Vinod is a bright, popular and well informed electronics engineer who graduated with an engineering degree from reputed college in June 2010. After his graduation he was out on many job interviews most of which he thought were courteous and reasonably useful in giving both his and prospective employer a fair impression of where each of them stood on matters of importance to both of them. It was therefore, with great anticipation that he looked forward to a one firm in which he most wanted to work, UML electronics ltd. He firmly believed that best use of his training and skills lay in working for a firm like UML electronics ltd, where he thought he could have a successful career.

The interview however was a digester. Vinod walked in to a room in which 3 members including President, Vice president and another engineer, Begin throwing questions at him that he felt were aimed primarily at tripping him up rather than finding out what he could offer through his engineering skills. The question ranges from unnecessarily discourteous to irrelevant like. Are you planning on settling down and starting a family any time soon? Then, after the interview, he was interviewed by two of the gentlemen exclusively (including the President) and the discussion focused almost exclusively on his technical expertise. He thought that these later discussions went fairly well. However, given the apparent aimlessness and even spiritedness of the panel interview, he was astonished when several days later he got the job offer from the firm.

The offer forced him to consider several matter. From his point of view, the job its self was perfect. He liked what he would be doing, the industry and the firm's location. And in fact, the president had been quite courteous in subsequent discussions, as had been the other member of the management team. He was left wondering whether the panel interview had been intentionally tense to see how he would stand up under the presser and if so, why they would do such a thing.

## Discussions

1. Do you think the panel interview reflected a well thought out the interview strategy on the part of the firm or carelessness on the part of the firm's management?

2. Would you take the job offer if you were Vinod? If you are not sure, is there any additional information that would help you makes your decision, and if so what is it?

# AN AUTOMATED PERFORMANCE APPRAISAL SYSTEM (APAS) AT STATE TRANSPORT CORPORATION

## Company Profile

State Transport Company Bangalore is a Semi Government organisation, having 18200 employees based across the state. The company was incorporated in the year 2002, with an objective to provide road goods transportation service. This transportation service is a serious business, and so it's no surprise that it's risky to work at the State Transport Company Bengaluru. The State Transport Company operates in 25 Districts of the state.

It is a family-owned company, known for employee friendly decisions and initiatives. Especially, it's a drivers dream in the state to join the company to do drivers job with satisfaction. Company had employee friendly policies, when it comes to promoting employee performance and job satisfaction. Like almost every smart company, State Transport Company recognizes that employees are more likely to stay with their employer when they feel connected and recognized for their efforts. Evaluation and performance management programs are critical to aligning corporate and employee values and priorities. The company followed a traditional yearly Performance appraisal system, outsourced to local consultants every year to make HR related decisions based on these recommendations. Recently, the company has realized that, their employee number has increased rapidly due to the growing business and the employee friendly policies of the company. As such, the company has realized that the old performance evaluation system is never the less appropriate and suitable to complete employee performance evaluation and appraisal within the stipulated time, and cost. Thus the company management has decided to overhaul and automate its traditional employee performance management process from the current performance year.

## The Challenge

State Transport Company's search for a new employee performance and talent management system began in 2012, when the company was divided into four branches of the transportation business. One branch introduced an automated performance appraisal (APAS) software program for its evaluation. Whereas the other branches were doing their employee performance appraisals manually using paper formats. The task of updating and consolidating the APAS process was assigned to a team of HR executives of the company headed by Mr. S.T. Patil, Manager, HRD, of State Transport Company's Head office at Bangalore. The team out of their research could find a single automated system that could be used for all of State transport company's 600 employees in four wings. The driving factor behind State Transport Company's APAS automation was the belief that thorough, accurate reviews help employees to better understand what's expected of them, so that they can set clear, measurable objectives. That translates into higher employee satisfaction, said Mr. S.T. Patil; of the State transport company's Manager for Human Resources Development. He says "When employees feel they have got a thorough and accurate review, it boosts their morale." It also leads to improved talent management and employee retention, which management experts know is a key factor in corporate growth and market leadership.

## Solution

To meet their strategic goals, Mr. Patil and his team drew up a list of the criteria that a new system had to meet. Top on the list was ease of use. Mr. Patil says "We didn't want to end up with a system that is so complicated that the managers wouldn't use it." A new system also had to save time. Because employees were in multiple locations, it needed to be web-based for accessibility. And it had to be flexible, easily incorporating core competencies into different forms. State Transport Company's selection committee looked at products from different software vendors. "We eliminated right away those that were geared to very large companies and those that were not web-based," Mr. Patil said. "We also eliminated those that offered too many options for customization. It's one thing to offer options, but another thing when the product requires so much customization that it becomes overwhelming."

The new automated employee performance appraisal system has completely formalized and organized State Transport Company's employee evaluation process. Mr. Patil said "It allows us to standardize competencies across job classifications, add signature and comment sections to make our process more interactive, and increase accessibility for remote managers."

The committee selected a web-based employee performance and talent management application developed by Karnataka Software solutions (KSS). "We liked the way it looked, and we really liked the user-friendliness of it. It's easy for the managers to use and it's customizable without overwhelming them," Mr. Patil said. After two days of training by KSS staff, four members of State Transport Company's team set out to train the company's supervisors on the new system. The company then trained 50 Depot Managers through a crash course in using e-Appraisal, and then used it to complete annual evaluations in May. State Transport Company's HR team is now customizing the software to include more relevant competencies and to respond to comments from managers and staff on the new system. Mr. Patil says that "The feedback has been really positive, from both managers and employees as well. Some staff said this was the best appraisal they've had." He further says that, they felt the evaluations were fair and realistic, and supervisors had the scope to provide more relevant and legitimate comments than they could before. Rather than just clicking on a bunch of canned comments, they were accurately reviewing the employee."

# Results

The new automated employee performance appraisal system (APAS) has completely formalized and organized State Transport Company's employee evaluation process. It has enabled the company to standardize competencies across job classifications, add signature and comment sections to make our process more interactive, and increase accessibility for remote managers. Under State Transport Company's old system, employees conducting reviews started from scratch once a year with new performance journals. KSS will let them log notes throughout the year and regularly update their on-line appraisals. Employees use one consistent form to add comments and to sign their appraisals.

The web-based product helps remote and traveling managers maintain access to the forms and the data they need to evaluate their staff. "In our old system, a few folks in Bangalore would have access to the system. But today we have managers across the state have access to the system. It's important that they can share the same forms across the board. The employees who are working on the road a lot or are working out of home offices, so having them be able to access this is a huge improvement for the company. The management of the company is now opining "Organizing and automating the appraisal process results in appraisals that are more accurate and fair. This is important because, after all, an employee appraisal is a legal document," The new system is also helping the company to elucidate training requirements and development in its staff. The company developed a separate training manual so that they can go in to the evaluations and more easily monitor employees' skills development, see what training is needed by individuals and check the due dates for training and renewal.

The new employee performance and talent management system has proven to be a big time-saver for State Transport Company's HR team. Since this year was the first time using the new system, it took us a little longer than it will next year. But the process was a whole lot faster. It has already saved a lot of time, and the HR Department was able to do everybody's appraisals in one shot. The new system is also helping the Company to better align employee activities with the company's business objectives.

# Discussions

1. "Automation in Appraisals will improvise the performance measurement," Justify

2. "Performance appraisal increases the employee morale and belief on the company's management" Agree or disagree?

3. The automation of the appraisal points out what type of performance appraisal method and how?

# MACHINIST'S INDISCIPLINE BEHAVIOR-1

Dinesh, a machine operator worked as a mechanist for Ganesh, the supervisor in an Iron works in Hubli, an upcoming Industry producing iron castings. There are 120 machinists working under 12 Supervisors, 3 Shift In charges (Engineers) and Two Production Managers. The Iron works has all three departments production, marketing and Finance working in the same factory premises at Belur Industrial area.

One day while supervising production Mr. Ganesh observed that, certain trash was fallen on floor unclean by the workers, in particular by the machinist Dinesh. While following up for the same, Ganesh told Dinesh to pick up some trash that had fallen from Dinesh's work area, and Dinesh replied, "I won't do the Janitor's work."

Ganesh replied, "When you drop it, you pick it up." Dinesh became angry and abusive, calling Ganesh a number of names in a loud voice and refusing to pick up the trash. All employees in the Department heard Dinesh's comments.

Ganesh had been trying for two weeks to get his employees to pick up trash in order to have cleaner workplace and prevent accidents. He talked to all employees in weekly departmental meeting and to each employee individually at least once. He stated that he was following the instructions of the general manager. The only objection came from Dinesh.

Dinesh has been with the company for five years, and in this department for six months. Ganesh had spoken to him twice about excessive alcoholism, but otherwise his record was good. He was known to have quick temper.

This outburst by Dinesh hurts Ganesh badly. Later supervisor called Dinesh to come to office and suspended him for one day for insubordination and abusive language to a supervisor. The decision was within company policy and similar behaviors had been punished in other departments.

After Dinesh left Ganesh's office, Ganesh phoned the HR Manager, reported what he had done, and said that he was sending a copy of the suspension order for Dinesh's file.

## Discussions

1. What is the morale of the story?

2. Is the punishment, made to the machinist is appropriate? Justify your answer

3. What alternative disciplinary action do you suggest against the machinist?

# MACHINIST'S INDISCIPLINE BEHAVIOUR-2

While taking the full feedback on the development of Dinesh's case, the HR manager called one of his colleagues Satish and enquired in person. Satish also described him the summary of the discussion happened after the incident.

At the end of the shift on Saturday, normally all the members of the informal group of employees who play volley ball sport at the factory Gymkhana setup by the company for the recreation of the employees. Dinesh was surrounded by few of his colleagues and was commented for his suspension.

Mr. Jadhav, another machinist expressed his dissatisfaction on the behavior of his supervisor and shift in-charge, and said they treat few of the subordinates whom they don't like as animals and play lot of discrimination in assigning work. The grievance expressed by Mr. Jadhav was very much alarming to other colleagues that, overtime duty and special duty will be given to only those who, give special treats to the supervisors and shift in-charge persons and overtime will not be uniformly distributed as it give double the routing wages.

Hanif and Lamani commented on the job based incentives paid last year were altogether biased and this year it is a challenge for the sufferers to claim equal chances. The promotions given were also involved with the personal bias made by the Shift in charges and production manager. The team was of the opinion that, this year also company will declare incentives, promotion, training and transfer of employees. They also suggested Dinesh to meet the HR manager personally and vacate his suspension otherwise it will be a record against his performance and may lose possible increments and incentives.

Few of the senior machinists seriously expressed his views in terms of the company's policy towards all the above is week and is not based on factual assessment of the performance of the employees. The company should revise its policy and establish a transparent system of assessing employee's performance and then make appropriate decision interms of incentives, increments and promotion. They expressed their dissatisfaction on the transfer and training policy also.

Listening to the briefing gave by Satish out of the overall discussion of the employees, the HR manager realized about the company's improper practice of performance appraisal, and need for a formalized and scientific system as early as possible.

## Discussions

1. Comment on the case from the point of view of Performance appraisal.

# WORK ETHICS AND CULTURE AT F.I. TECHNOLOGIES

Rakesh and Krishna both of them are engineering graduates under different streams from same college. Rakesh is a electronics engineer and Krishna is from computer science department. Both of them are close to each other from college days. After graduation Rakesh pursued MBA in Information Technology specialization where as Krishna joined as software engineer in F.I. Technology.

Due to reference given by Krishna in his company Rakesh also got job in F.I. Technology after his masters. Both of them are working in same project with different responsibilities. Rakesh was interacting with clients of the company as he was business analyst of the project. By nature Krishna is friendly and ready to help the needy. Rakesh is silent, ethical and workaholic in nature ready to help if approached. A project manager was very happy about both of them as they are the constant performers from four years. Due to the job profile of Rakesh he was interacting with all the department of the company frequently.

Rakesh was given an additional responsibility to recruit new team members for the project, in which Krishna was also a member. Among many applicants ten are shortlisted by Krishna with different rounds of interview, in consultation with HR executive. The applicants list was send to Rakesh for next round of interview in which Krishna's wife Sneha name was also there. After the detailed interview done by Rakesh, he recommended only four potential applicants for final selection, in which Sneha name was not present. In the comments box Rakesh mentioned that "Sneha's skills are not matching with present requirements of the project. But in future she may be contacted if suitable vacancies are notified."

After a week project manager was surprised to see the resignation mail from Krishna. On the same day afternoon project manage met Krishna and Rakesh separately in cafeteria. After a brief discussion project manager opened a topic of resignation with Krishna. Few minutes later Krishna explained the reason for his resignation and behavior of Rakesh towards recruitment process. Project manager do not want to lose both of them as they are the constant performers in the team. At the same time project manager is very much confident that he will resolve the issue and retain both of them as he had understood the reason of the problem.

## Discussions

1. Discuss the ethical issues involved in the case.

2. If you are in the position of Rakesh, what is your stand on the situation?

3. Identify the issues involved in the case. If you are given a chance to resolve the issue what are your recommendations.

# ONLINE FOOD DELIVERY START-UP COMPANY

Rajashekhar, 22-year-old engineering student graduated from premier institute. Like other engineering students, he worked with Multi-national companies for about 5 years. Later he decided to chase his vision of opening his own company. In 2014, he started a start-up online food delivery company along with his wife and two relatives. His wife is also engineering graduate from same college. Post engineering, she worked for an IT company for 3 years and then taken a career break. His two relatives are from his native and both have completed graduation. Currently both of them are working with MNC companies in Sales field. Both of his relatives come with 10 years of Marketing and Sales experience of FMCG industry.

Rajashekhar & team named the company as 'FD'-Food Delivery. It is an online platform, where customer orders food of his/her choice from the selected menu and ordered food is packed and delivered at customer doorstep. In span of a year into the market, his company could able to draw list of customers. For first two years, Rajashekhar, as a CEO of the company managed with few employees, and with his wife managing kitchen and relatives managing the packaging, Operations and Logistics, which includes taking the order, packing and on time delivery.

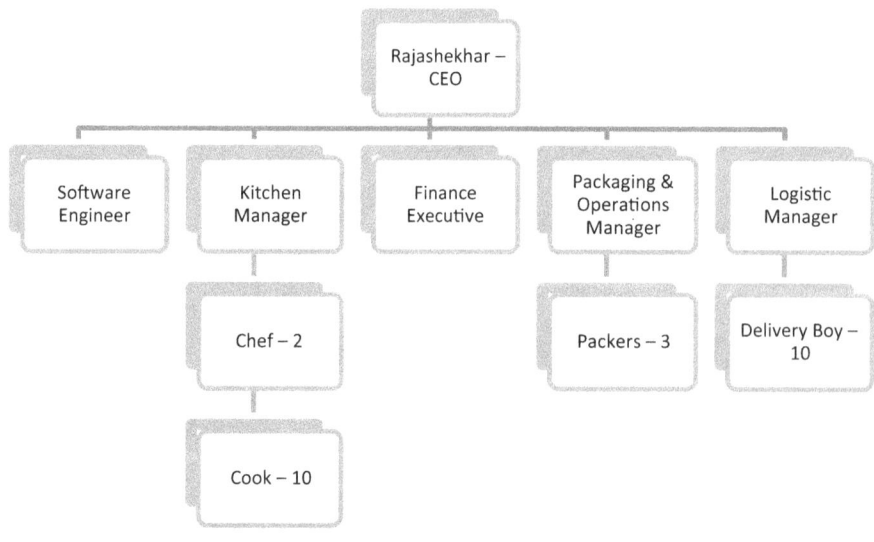

**Chart No. 01:** Organisation structure, 2014–15

First year of operations has witnessed 600% growth in customer base and 233% in the second year.

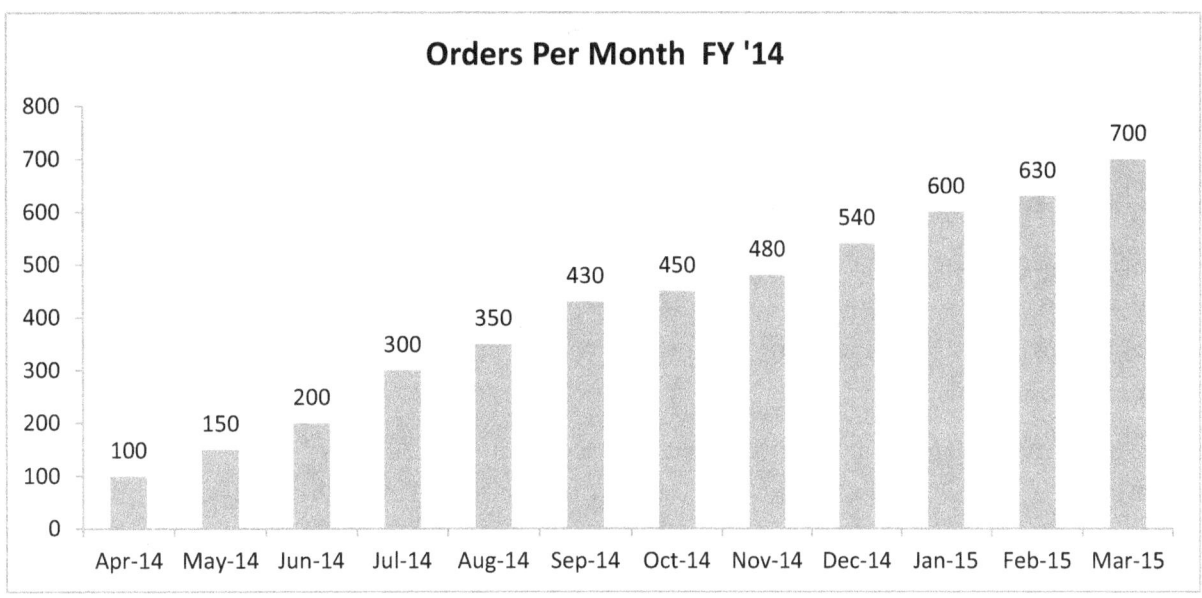

**Graph No. 1:** Orders served per month, 2014–15

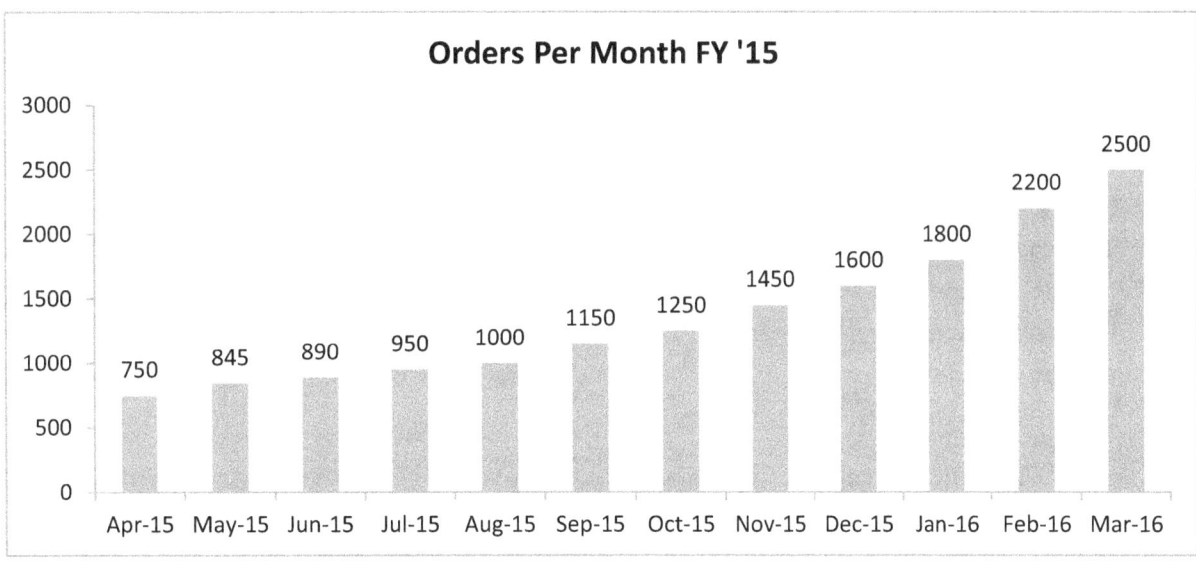

**Graph No. 2:** Orders served per month, 2015–16

His company raised million dollars in funding from impressive investors and emerged as the successful start-up company. Company also signed agreements with 1000 restaurants. These restaurants offer menu on the FD web/app, customer can order food of his/her choice. Then delivery team of FD will pick the food from the restaurant and deliver it to customer.

However, as the company started growing, employee base also started growing from four to a company with 100+ employees, and people at Managerial level to top executives to manage day-to-day operations. Rajashekhar did not like too many layers in the structure. He thought extra layer of supervision is just unnecessary, also an obstruction to day-to-day operations. However due to business exigencies, he had no option to create layers.

He recruited one of the experts from the food industry to procure grocery, vegetables, packaging materials and any other materials required for the company. He made him the head of procurements and asked him to form his team to manage the activities. Within few months, procurement head formed the team of 5 team leaders and 20 support staffs. Out of five recruited employees, two for procuring grocery, two to procure vegetables on daily basis and one for procuring packaging and any other materials for the company. Their profile includes, searching for best vendors in the market, who can supply the required quantity of groceries and vegetables with required quality at best price.

To manage complete IT solutions, CEO recruited one of his friends as head of IT. His friend is currently working with one of the well-known IT Company based in USA. Profile includes manage online platform, improvisation, and managing IT infrastructure of the company. He formed team of 2 team leaders and 10 engineers.

To manage marketing activities, CEO recruited another friend of him, who studied engineering with him and later he did his Master in Business Administration. His profile includes, online marketing to create awareness about the FD, track app download, print ads, customer feedback, and customer loyalty. He formed team of 2 team leaders and 10 marketing executives.

Growing number of people in the organisation has brought HR head and a team of 10 executives to manage recruitment, compensation and other activities.

Rajashekhar's wife manages kitchen. She has a team of 2 chefs and 20 Cooks. Rajashekhar's two relatives manage entire delivery section, which includes taking the order from online, packing and delivering it to customer doorsteps. Packaging and logistics team comprises of 5 packers and 15 delivery boys. Basic requirement to become delivery boy is to possess valid driving license and completed matriculation (10th Standard) with 18 years of age. The compensation includes fixed salary of Rs. 8000 and incentive basis the slab achievement. Every day, Rajashekhar, his wife and two relatives meet at the office in the morning to discuss and review the performance of the company. In spite of bigger team, CEO interacts with all staffs starting from procurement executives to chef to Cook to delivery boys. Sometimes he used to interact with ground staffs and take decisions without keeping respective department heads in loop.

5thApril 2017, in the annual meeting Rajashekhar presented the journey of the company with his expectations for year 2017.

**Table No. 1:** Company performance from 2014 to 2016 and Projection for 2017 & Beyond

| Particulars | 2014 | 2015 | 2016 | 2017 | 2018 | 2019 |
|---|---|---|---|---|---|---|
| Average Order Value | 350 | 450 | 550 | 650 | 700 | 750 |
| Gross Margin | 6% | 8% | 9% | 10% | 10% | 10% |
| Delivery Cost | 60 | 60 | 55 | 53 | 55 | 55 |
| Other cost | 25 | 25 | 15 | 12 | 13 | 10 |
| Net Revenue | -64 | -49 | -23 | 0 | 2 | 10 |

His vision is to start making profit from 2018. He says to the team that, "As a company we need to maintain customer base, increase average order value, increase the margin and reduce cost so that we can start making profit from 2018."

Later in the year 2017, online food delivery market witnessed huge competition from other small and large players. This also called for challenges. Emergence of e-commerce offered plenty of choices for customer leading to uncertainty in the loyalty. A company that provides better price deals, discounts, freebies earns the customer loyalty.

During quarterly review meeting on 1-July-2017, marketing head presented the data, which is not a good sign for the company. For every order served, company collects customer feedback on a rating scale of 5. The average overall rating in 2015 was at 5.00, whereas it has come down to 3.4 by the end of Q1–2017.

**Table No. 2:** Customer Rating 2015 to Q1 2017

| | 2015 | 2016 | Q1- 2017 |
|---|---|---|---|
| Quality of Food | ★★★★★ | ★★★⯨☆ | ★★★☆☆ |
| Pricing | ★★★★★ | ★★★★★ | ★★★⯨☆ |
| Packaging | ★★★★★ | ★★★★★ | ★★★★☆ |
| On time delivery | ★★★★★ | ★★★★⯨ | ★★★☆☆ |
| Overall Rating | ★★★★★ | ★★★★☆ | ★★★⯨☆ |

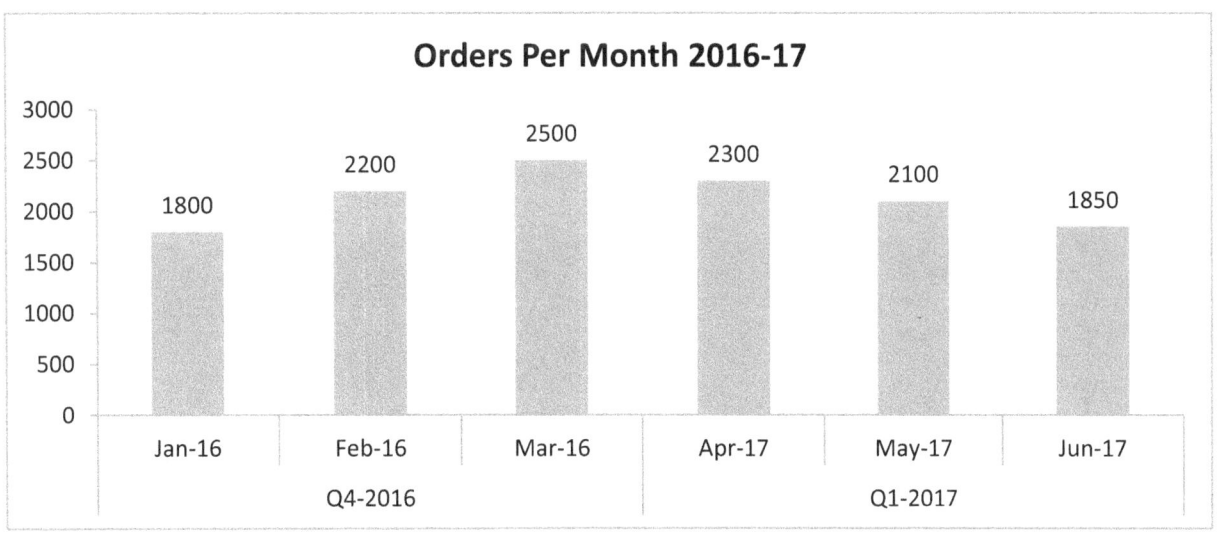

**Graph No. 3:** Orders served per month trend, Comparison between Q4 '16 vs Q1' 17

This report did not go well with wife and two relatives of Rajashekhar, CEO. Logistics head presented the following report.

## Business Potentiality

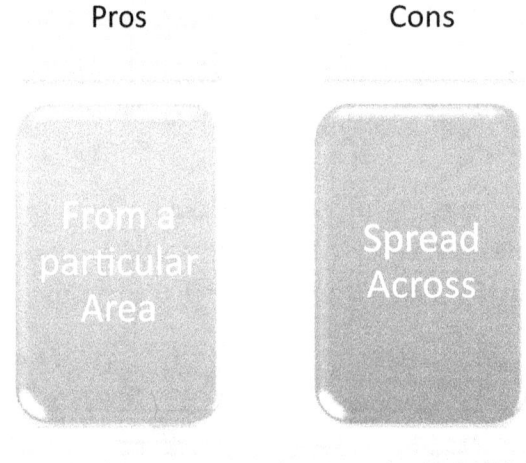

## Delivery Area

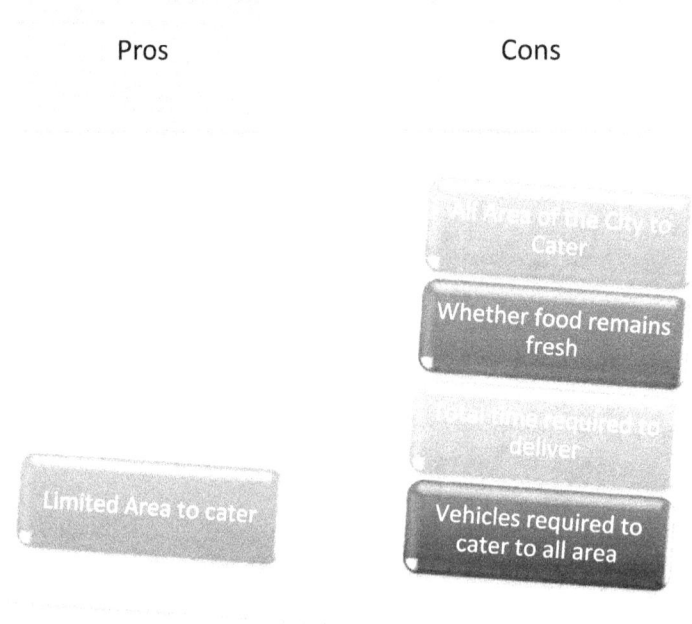

From a particular area – It means business comes from a particular area of the city.

Spread across – It means business is spread across different locations of the city.

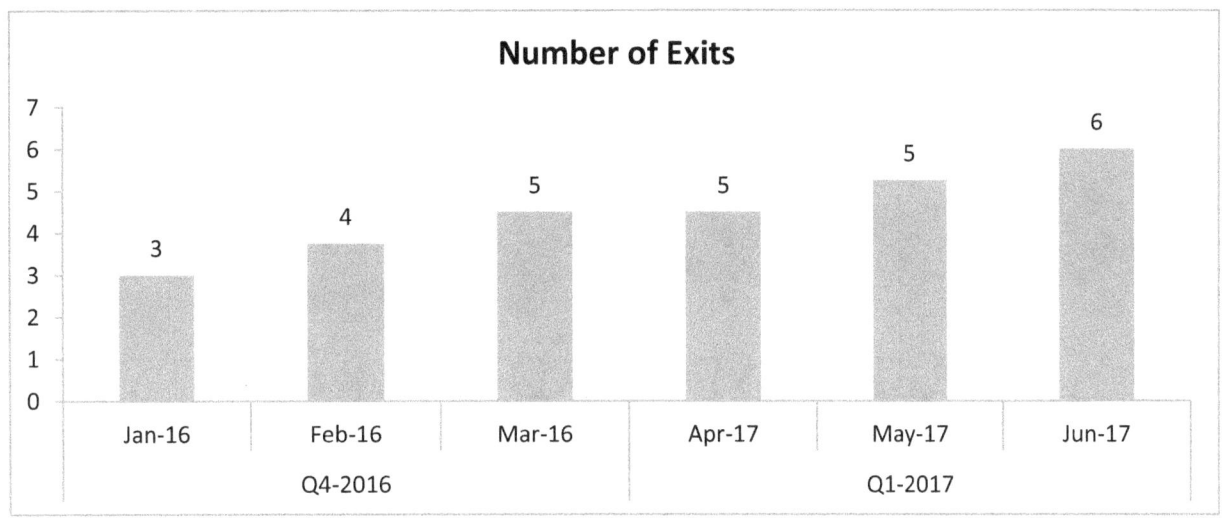

**Graph No. 4:** Number of Exits, Comparison between Q4'16 vs Q1'17

Logistics head said, in spite of many efforts to retain, there is huge attrition in delivery boys. Because of this reason, there is a hit in the delivery time hence the rating has gone down.

Head Kitchen started blaming procurement department for sourcing poor quality grocery and vegetables. In addition, there is huge attrition in chefs and cooks. She said there is dearth for availability of quality and qualified chefs and cooks. There is inconsistency in the food delivered by restaurants with which company has the tie up.

CEO said to meet our 2018 objective and looking at the spike in customer base, it becomes important for the company to strengthen our operations, logistics, kitchen, vendors, and marketing activity. He felt, there is a need to restructure and relook at the strategies and approaches adopted by Human resources department, marketing department and company as a whole.

# APPAREL-READYMADE GARMENTS COMPANY

'Apparel' is a readymade garment company located in industrial area of Bangalore. In 1960, company started as a small-scale industry. Company is into Men & Women readymade garments. Apparel Company gets the order from leading companies. Company started with employee base of 50, and it has grown to 1000 employees by 2017. This industry requires people with expertise in sourcing, manufacturing, business development and sales.

Organisation structure of the company is as follows –**Top Management**

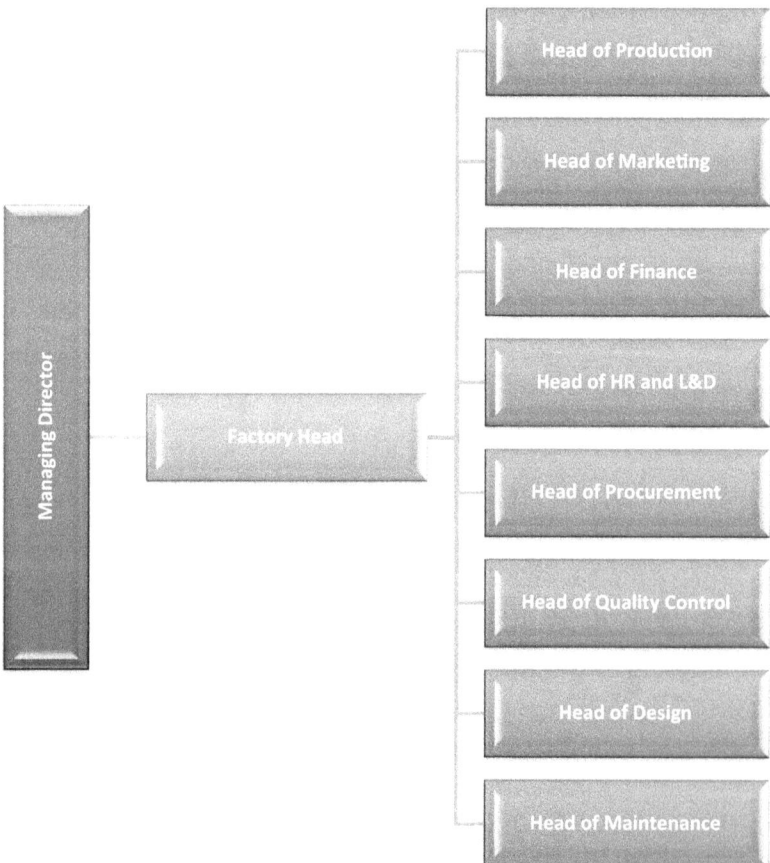

1. Department wise structure – **Production Department**

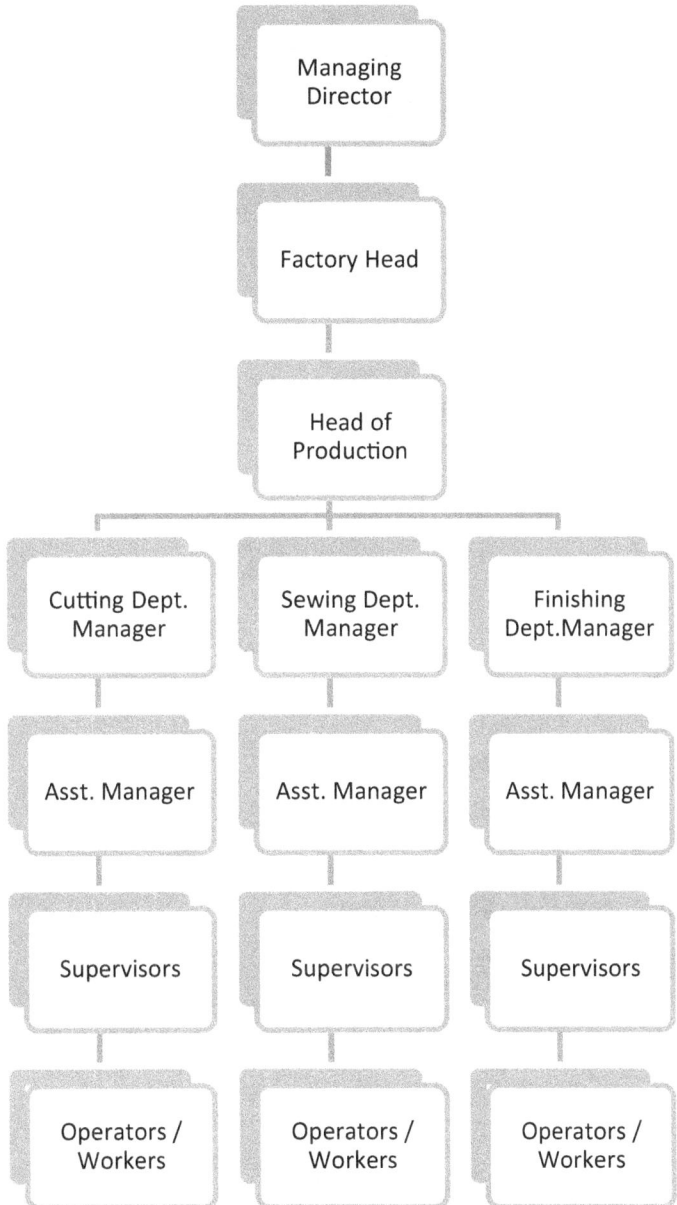

**Employee Strength of the department:**

| Production Department | |
|---|---|
| Head of Production | 1 |
| Cutting Dept. Manager | 1 |
| Sewing Dept. Manager | 1 |
| Finishing Dept. Manager | 1 |
| Asst. Manager | 10 |
| Supervisors | 50 |
| Operators/Workers – On Contract | 2500 |

2. Department wise structure – **Marketing Department**

**Employee Strength of the department:**

| Marketing Department | |
|---|---|
| Head of Marketing | 1 |
| Manager | 2 |
| Executives | 10 |

3. Department wise structure – **Design & Sampling Department**

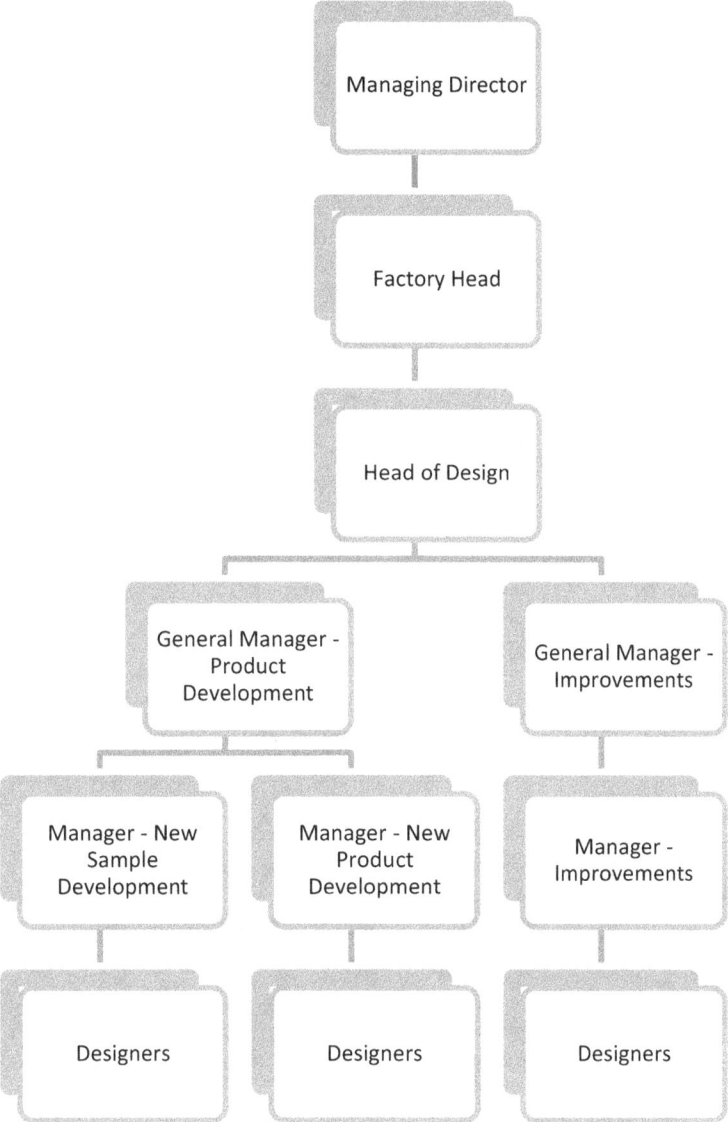

**Employee Strength of the department:**

| Design & Sampling Department | |
|---|---|
| Head of Design | 1 |
| General Manager – Product Development | 1 |
| General Manager – Improvements | 1 |
| Manager – New Sample Development | 1 |
| Manager – New Product Development | 1 |
| Manager – Improvements | 1 |
| Designers – Sample Development | 5 |
| Designers – New Product Development | 10 |
| Designers – Improvements | 5 |

4.  Department wise structure – **Finance Department**

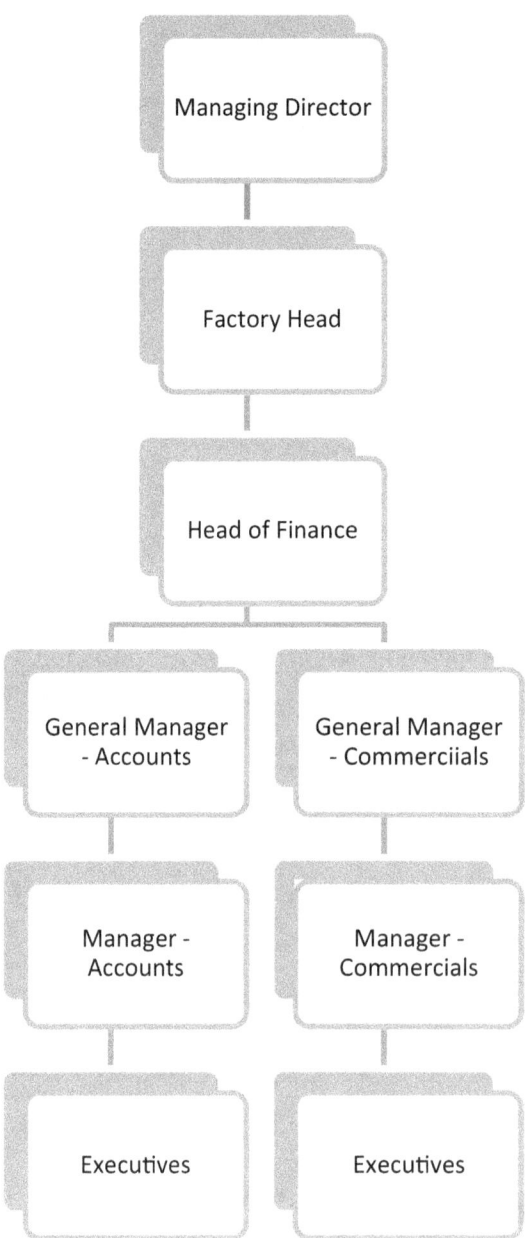

**Employee Strength of the department:**

| Finance Department | |
|---|---|
| Head of Finance | 1 |
| General Manager – Accounts | 1 |
| General Manager – Commercials | 1 |
| Manager – Accounts | 1 |
| Manager – Commercials | 1 |
| Executives – Accounts | 12 |
| Executives – Commercials | 4 |

5. Department wise structure – **HR and L&D Department**

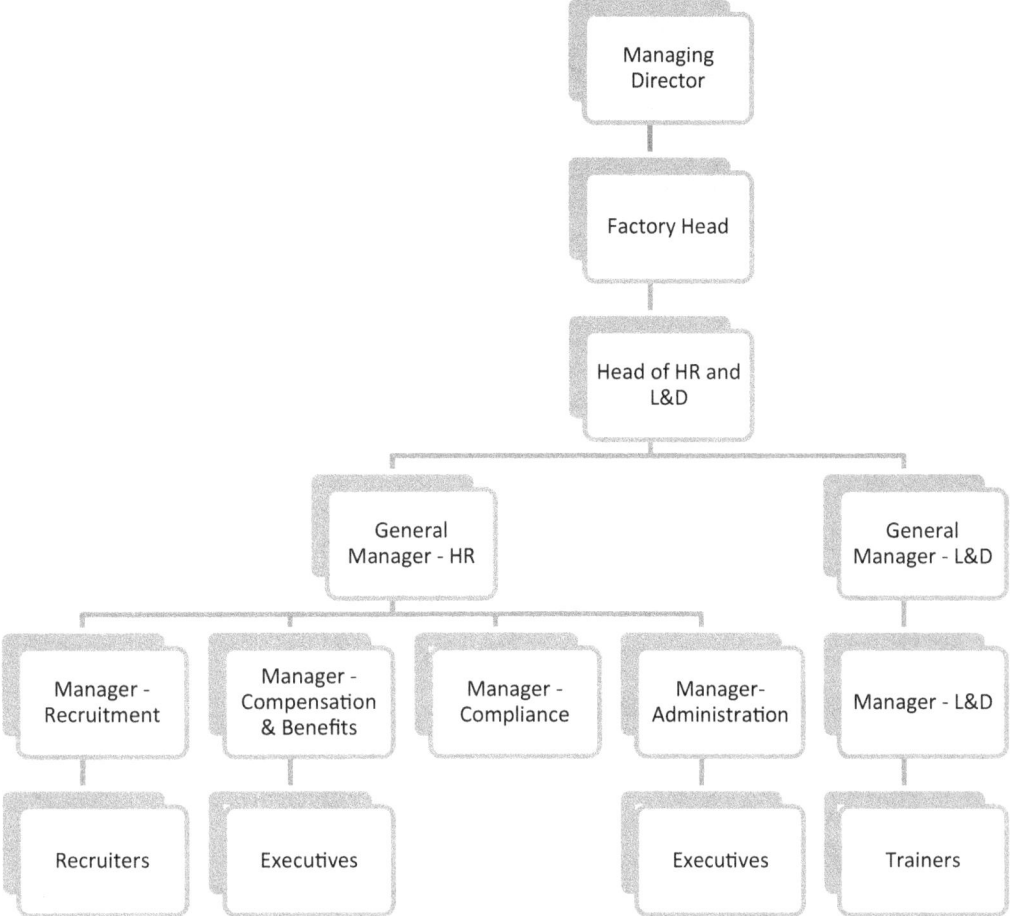

## Employee Strength of the department:

| HR and L&D Department | |
|---|---|
| Head of HR and L&D | 1 |
| General Manager – HR | 1 |
| General Manager – L&D | 1 |
| Manager – Recruitment | 1 |
| Manager – Compensation & Benefits | 1 |
| Manager – Compliance | 1 |
| Manager – Administrations | 1 |
| Manager – L&D | 1 |
| Recruiters | 10 |
| Executives – Compensation & Benefits | 5 |
| Executives – Administrations | 2 |
| Trainers | 4 |

6. Department wise structure – **Procurement Department**

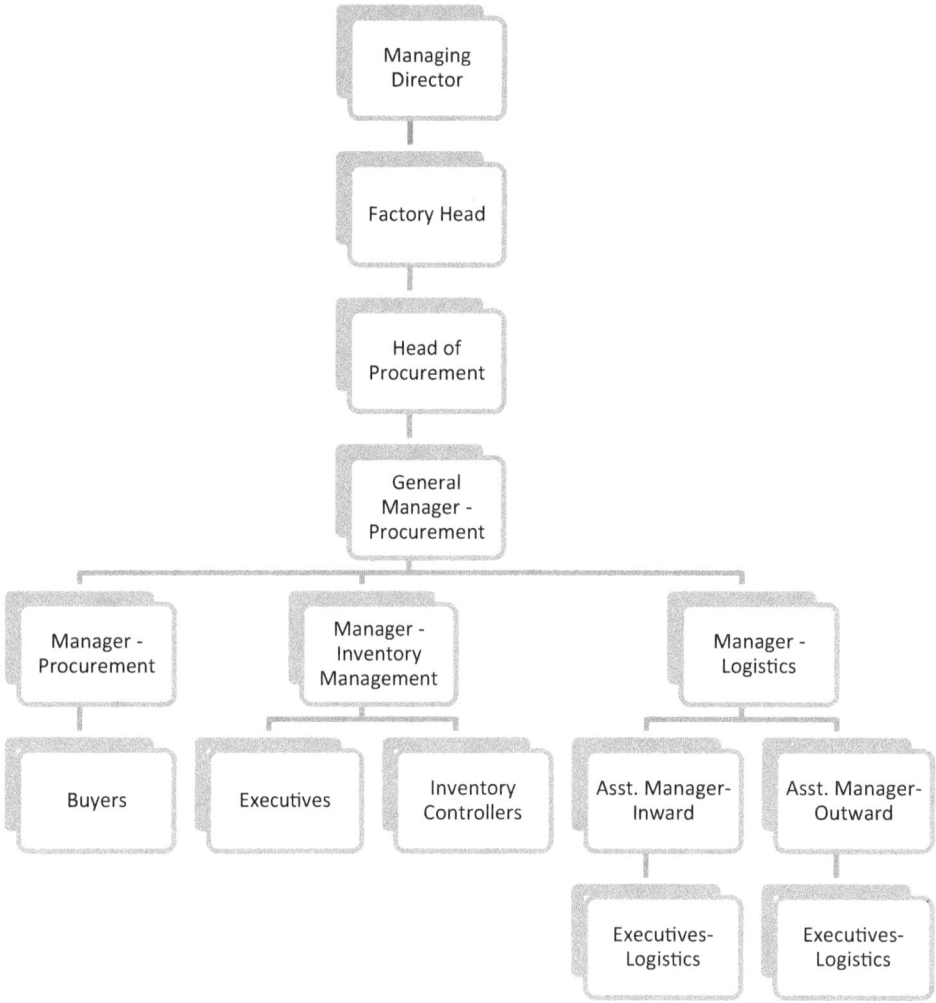

**Employee Strength of the department:**

| Procurement Department | |
|---|---|
| Head of Procurement | 1 |
| General Manager – Procurement | 1 |
| Manager – Procurement | 1 |
| Manager – Inventory Management | 1 |
| Manager – Logistics | 1 |
| Buyers | 15 |
| Executives – Inventory Management | 1 |
| Executives – Inventory Controllers | 1 |
| Assistant Manager – Inwards | 1 |
| Assistant Manager – Outwards | 1 |
| Executives – Logistics | 10 |

7. Department wise structure – **Quality Control Department**

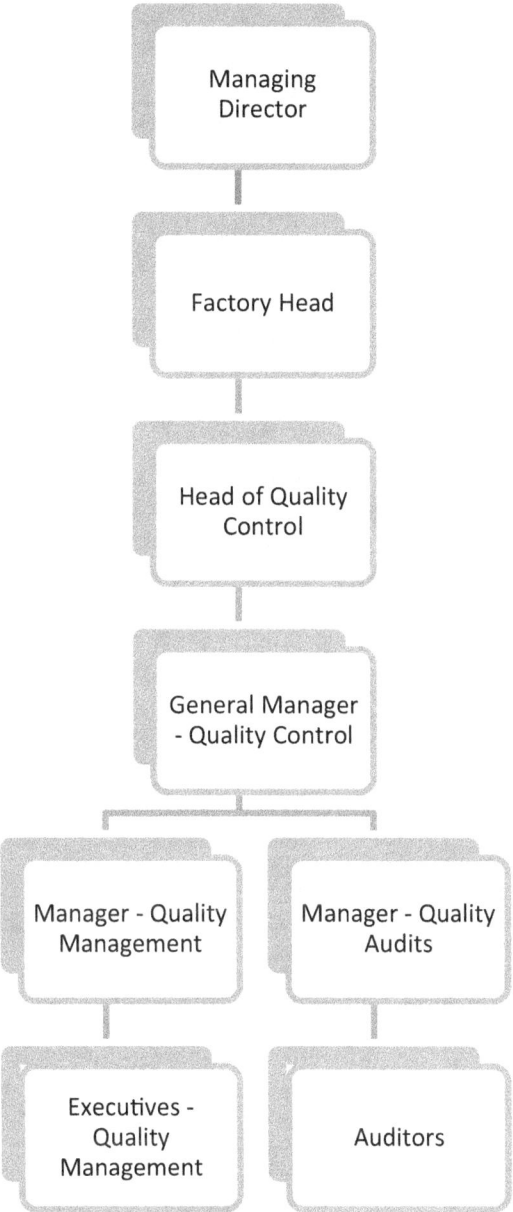

**Employee Strength of the department:**

| Quality Control Department | |
|---|---|
| Head of Quality Control | 1 |
| General Manager – Quality Control | 1 |
| Manager – Quality Control | 2 |
| Manager – Quality Audits | 1 |
| Executives – Quality Management | 25 |
| Auditors | 5 |

8.  Department wise structure – **Maintenance Department**

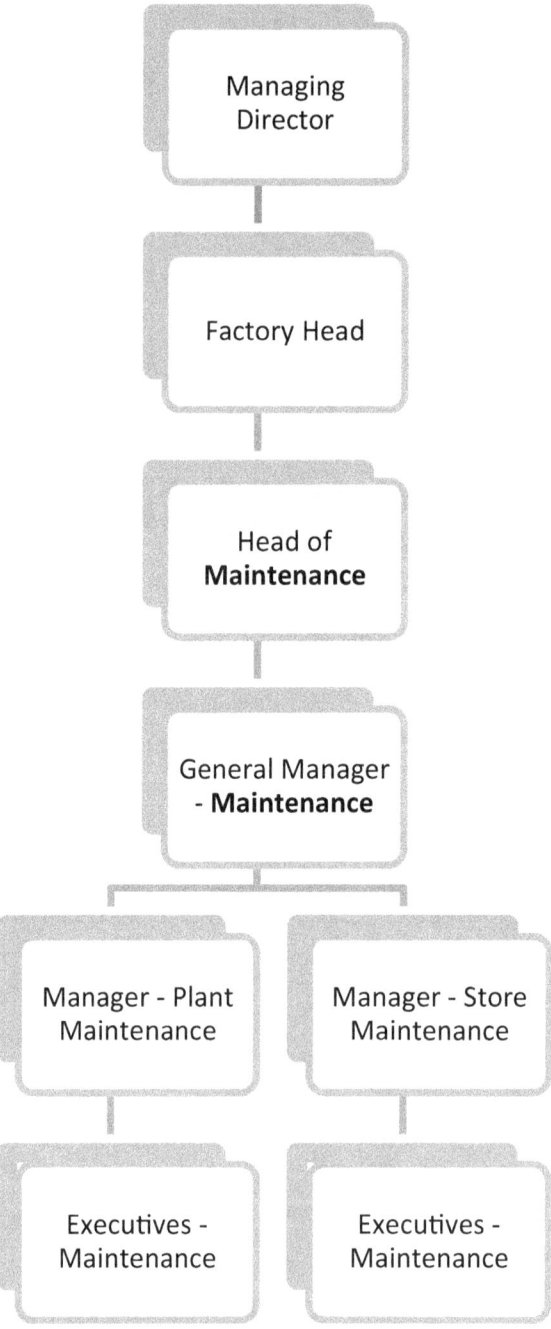

**Employee Strength of the department:**

| Maintenance Department | |
|---|---|
| Head of Maintenance | 1 |
| General Manager – Maintenance | 1 |
| Manager – Plant Maintenance | 2 |
| Manager – Store Maintenance | 1 |
| Executives – Maintenance | 15 |

Following graphs show male-female ratio of the company

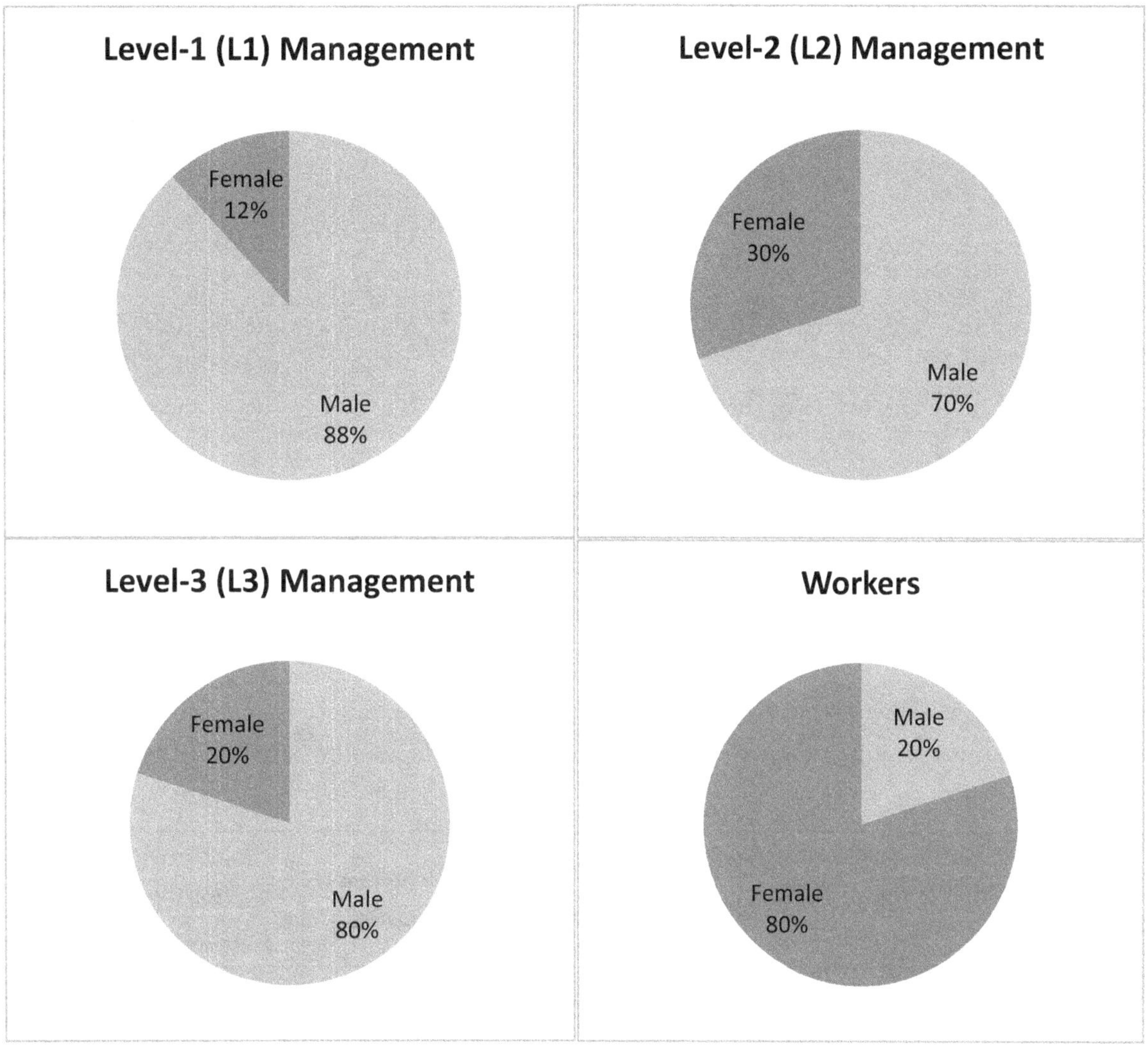

## Level-1 (L1) Management

Female
12%

Male
88%

## Level-2 (L2) Management

Female
30%

Male
70%

## Level-3 (L3) Management

Female
20%

Male
80%

## Workers

Male
20%

Female
80%

Levels defined as follows by the company:

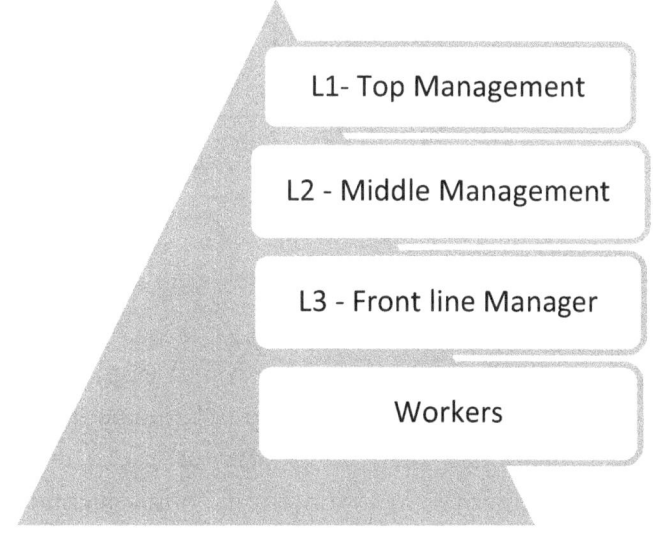

L1- Top Management

L2 - Middle Management

L3 - Front line Manager

Workers

In the annual company meeting, Human Resource department of the company has shared a report to top management of the company in which it highlights some of top management and people holding key positions are nearing retirements.

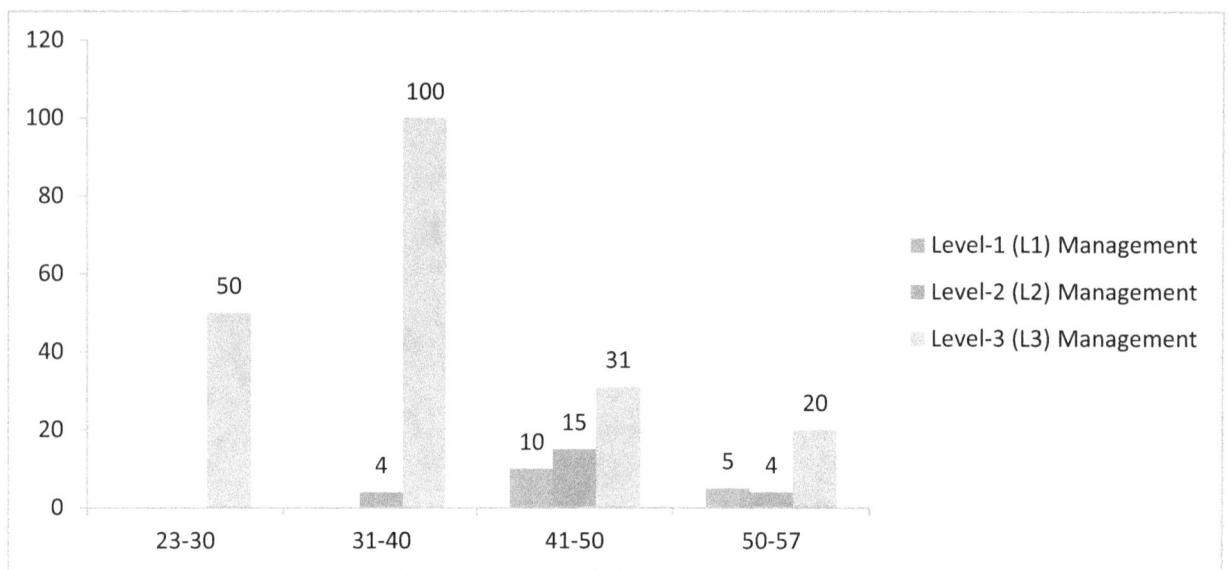

In the meeting, to a query by one of the HOD, L&D Head says, 80% of the training is on functional and around 20% on soft-skills training. The major gap is the competency based and career development programs.

| Levels | Product Training | | Process Training | | Machine Related Training | | Safety Training | | System Training | | Role Specific Training | | Soft Skill Training | |
|---|---|---|---|---|---|---|---|---|---|---|---|---|---|---|
| | CRT | OJT | CRT | OJT | CRT | OJT | CRT | OJT | CRT | OJT | CRT | OJT | CRT | E-Learning |
| Level-1 (L1) Management | | | | | | | | | | | | | | ✓ |
| Level-2 (L2) Management | | | | | | | ✓ | | ✓ | | | ✓ | | ✓ |
| Level-3 (L3) Management | ✓ | | | | ✓ | | ✓ | | | | ✓ | ✓ | | |
| Workers | | ✓ | | ✓ | | ✓ | | ✓ | | | | | | |

| |
|---|
| CRT – Classroom Training |
| OJT – On the Job Training |

Head of Production department brings forth a case of a woman employee to the meeting. He says that, recently few selected women staff approached him with a complaint about a supervisor. In the complaint, three women employees have mentioned that, the Supervisor passes offensive comments regarding appearance and clothes of woman employees, and unwelcome physical conduct of sexual nature. When this case was brought to notice of front-line managers and HR executives, a verbal warning issued. This supervisor has some political background and a relative of the contractor who supplies work force to the company. Due to this harassment, women employees are not able to concentrate on daily duties & responsibilities.

There is another friend of this supervisor, who speaks disrespectfully and uses abusive language with the employees. He is the relative of one of leading vendors, who gives company 30% of the business. In both the cases, workers are afraid to complaint about them, as they feel they may lose their job.

In the Audit report, Head of Quality Control Department highlighted the concern of poor quality material procurement. He says, during one of the audits conducted by the auditor, it was observed that, procurement department did not follow certain processes. If recorded, then these would be considered as non-compliance for the Company & would result in heavy penalty. When the auditor pointed it out, the Procurement Manager offered a favor in return for not recording the same in the audit feedback.

In the conclusion, Managing Director of the company instructs Head of HR and L&D to prepare a detailed action & execution plan on the following area.

a. Succession planning

b. Programs around Productivity enhancement

c. Working conditions of workers specially women

d. Code of Conduct/Ethical issues viz, Integrity of some buyers/procurement staffs, Exploitation by vendors with contract staffs.

# ANNEXURE

**Times of India, 20.01.2018**

Times of India, 20.01.2018

**Times of India, 26.01.2018**

**Times of India, 26.01.2018**

**Times of India, 26.01.2018**

**Times of India, 26.01.2018**

Times of India, 26.01.2018

**Times of India, 26.01.2018**

**Times of India, 10.02.2018**

# REFERENCES

1. Audit Bureau of Circulations (ABC). (2017). print media is growing – 2.37 crore copies added in the last 10 years, Press release, May 2017

2. EY and RAI, Pulse of Indian retail market, A survey of CFOs in the Indian retail sector, Ernst & Young LLP and Retailers Association of India (RAI), March 2014.

3. Exchange4media News Service. (2015)S-Group Insights: Print Ads See 19% Growth In Top Retail Categories, Radio Ads Rise 12%, Available: https://www.exchange4media.com/Advertising/ S-Group-InsightsPrint-ads-see-19-growth-in-top-retail-categories-radio-ads-rise-12_61834.html, September 2015.

4. India Brand Equity Foundation (IBEF).(2017), Retail, *IBEF Report.*1–51.

5. India Brand Equity Foundation (IBEF).(2018). https://www.ibef.org/industry/ecommerce.aspx.

6. KPMG India-FICCI. (2017). Media for the Masses: The Promise Unfolds. Indian Media and Entertainment Industry Report, Page 1–294, 2017.

7. Mohit Bansal and Shubham Gupta (2014), Impact of Newspaper Advertisement on Consumer Behavior, Global Journal of Finance and Management, ISSN 0975–6477 Volume 6, Number 7 (2014), pp. 669–674.

8. www.wikipedia.org/w/index.php?title=Ketan_Parekh

9. http://indiansharemarketinfotips.blogspot.in

10. www.nseindia.com.

11. www.bseindia.com.

12. SEBI Guidelines and information

13. Business world magazine

14. Many leading news papers, websites and business articles and case study books etc are referred for secondary data.

15. USDA Foreign Agricultural Service, GAIN Report, Global Agricultural Information Network, 2/20/2015, Page 1–15.

16. Times of India and other leading news papers.

www.ingramcontent.com/pod-product-compliance
Lightning Source LLC
Chambersburg PA
CBHW081238180526
45171CB00005B/464